A FAR OFF SUNLIT PLACE

*The Life and Times of John Sutherland, Neurologist,
of Scotland and Australia.*

John MacKay Sutherland

Amphion Press
1989

A FAR OFF SUNLIT PLACE
The Life and Times of John Sutherland, Neurologist,
of Scotland and Australia.

Bibliography
Illustrations
Appendices
Notes and References
Includes Index

1st Edition (English)
First Published   1989

Typeset & Published by: Amphion Press, The Department of Child Health, Royal Children's Hospital, Brisbane, Queensland, 4029, Australia.

Printed by: Merino Lithographics, 18 Baldock Street, Moorooka, Brisbane, Queensland 4105, Australia.

Cover by: Paul Ramsden, The Queensland Museum.

  John MacKay Sutherland

CATALOGUING IN PUBLICATION DATA
National Library of Australia
Sutherland, John MacKay, 1919-
A Far Off Sunlit Place

1. Sutherland, John M. (John MacKay),
1919–   . 2. Neurologists – Australia – Biography.
3. Neurologists – Scotland – Biography. I. Title.
616.8'0092'4
NATIONAL LIBRARY OF AUSTRALIA CARD NUMBER AND ISBN
ISBN   0 86776 330 2.

FRONTISPIECE

Dr JOHN MACKAY SUTHERLAND

*Photograph, 1986, St Vincent's Hospital, Toowoomba,
courtesy of Mr David Seeto.*

FOR PAT

with whom these memories are shared.

CONTENTS

Contents

FOREWORD

As they grow older, and recognise the constraints life has increasingly imposed on their personal futures, some thinking men come to look back on their past with heightened interest and affection. They are able to see what has gone before in a clearer perspective and in relation to a wider and ripened view of things. At this time some are blessed with the energy, and the gift of words, that enables them to convert their mature thoughts and their recollections and appreciations of events and of men into a written record that can bring some measure of pleasure both to themselves and to others, particularly to those who have known them and to some extent shared in their times.

— It is from such a standpoint that John Sutherland has written an account of his days, rooted in a Celtic heritage, their first half spent amid cultures in some respects unfamiliar, yet not foreign, to that of the almost antipodean land in which he has now lived and worked for almost a third of a century. Perhaps, at least to the contemporary Australian reader, the interest in the book will lie as much in the glimpses it gives of a pre-War Scottish boyhood, and of Scottish professional life in the early years after World War II, as in the account of Queensland medicine and medical personalities in more recent times.

Perhaps the charm of the book will be found to derive from its genesis, the intention to provide grandchildren born into a distant and rather different world with some appreciation of their heritage. In many ways John Sutherland has written for all his readers with the consideration he would show his children (and he has many intellectual offspring in Australian neurological medicine). True to his nature, he has depicted events in a generous and unfailingly cheerful light, brushing over the frustrations and sadnesses, showing little of that attitude of mind about which Yeates wrote and which can so easily overtake those who look to the past:

Foreword

 Our shadows rove the garden gravel still,
The living seem more shadowy than they.

W.B. Yeates
These Old Shades

Those who have known John Sutherland only in his Australian days can now see the man more clearly against his background, and feel gratitude for his resurrecting another world for us as well as kindling memories of more recent times, even as we feel gratitude for all that he accomplished in Australian neurological medicine.

M.J. Eadie

PREFACE

I set out to write this account of my family solely for my grand-daughters, Jennifer and Louise McKee. Both were born in Australia and could not be expected at their age to have knowledge of or an interest in their Scottish ancestors other, hopefully, than their mother and maternal grandparents!

Yet, as Sir Iain Moncreiffe has pointed out in his Introduction to Noel Currer-Briggs and Royston Gambier's *Debrett's Family Historian* —

> ... *never forget that you each owe your very existence not just to your parents, but to every single one of your personal ancestors since mankind began ... you could never have been born if your mother's mother's mother's mother had died in infancy ... It would have been no good your direct maternal great-great grandfather marrying somebody else instead, because the child of such a marriage would have been quite different genetically from your real great-grandmother, and no descendants could ever have been you!*

By the age one becomes interested in one's ancestors, where and how they lived and their fortunes and misfortunes, although a genealogical tree may be constructed from government, census, parish and other records, it is often difficult to uncover any personal accounts of the lives they led.

It was with these thoughts in mind that I set about having my family tree traced and writing a personal account of our Caithness heritage, of our Celtic ancestors of 5,000 BC from the eastern Mediterranean, and of later ethnic tides which brought further Celtic settlers from the coasts of northern France, Brittany and Spain, and around 790-800 AD in their longships from northern Europe, the Vikings.

Preface

Knowledge of personal ancestors dates from shortly after the disastrous 1745 rebellion which ended on Culloden moor and which was followed by the subjugation of the Highlands and the consequent infamous 'clearances'. From this start I have attempted to describe something of the lives of the various generations including my own, my schooldays, University life and extracurricular activities, with a note of certain contemporary world events to give the story perspective.

At this stage entered my friend Professor M.J. Eadie, who suggested that I enlarge the work into an autobiography. I have tried to do this and apologise for the intrusion of a considerable amount of medical matters into Part II. My excuse for doing so is the important part the development of the Neurology Unit at the Royal Brisbane Hospital played in my professional life and for those interested in such matters I felt an account of the early years of the Department should be put on record.

Probably the best description of the book is 'a smattering of everything ... ' .

John M. Sutherland

ACKNOWLEDGEMENTS ....

My wife, Pat, and Mrs Janet Wickham typed and repeatedly retyped the manuscript. Without their expert assistance, patience and support, this project could not have come to fruition.

I am grateful to Mrs Rosemary Bigwood, MA, MLitt., genealogist, of Edinburgh who carried out the research into my family.

The superb photographs of Orkney are the work of Mr Charles Tait of Charles Tait Photographic, Kelton, St Ola, Orkney. My thanks are due to the Photography Unit, Royal Naval Air Station, Gosport, for the helicopter photograph. I wish to thank particularly Mr Graham Jurott, (Clinical Photographer, The Faculty of Medicine, University of Queensland) whose photographic expertise made the illustration of this book possible, and Mr Paul Ramsden of the Queensland Museum for employing his artistic skills in designing the cover of the book.

Mr Clifford Hanley, author, historian and broadcaster of Glasgow, who wrote the lyrics of *Scotland the Brave*, generously gave me permission to use *A Far Off Sunlit Place* as my title and to quote from his lyrics. The gaelic rendering of the title is also due to Mr Hanley — although not entirely his own work! As he puts it, 'We are indebted to a nice lassie in the BBC for this'. I am grateful to her.

In the Appendices I have acknowledged the assistance of authors whose works have been referred to and who, in particular, made the early chapters possible. I apologise for any omission which may inadvertently have occurred.

I am deeply indebted to Dr Malcolm and Mrs Gail White of Melbourne, and the Malong Trust, for generous support in the publication of this book; and to Mr Charles Scandrett and Staff, Printers, of Merino Lithographics, for encouragement and the excellent quality of that firm's work.

Acknowledgements

It is a pleasure to thank Professor M.J. Eadie for the Foreword. As I have indicated in the Preface he is largely responsible for the book and I am grateful to him for support and practical help throughout its preparation.

Finally, without the encouragement and expertise of my publisher Professor John Pearn and his publishing officer, Mrs Peggy Carter, of the Department of Child Health, University of Queensland, this book could not have been published in its present form. I am most grateful to them and thank them sincerely for their forbearance and for the care they have taken in the preparation of this volume.

PART I

BENEATH SCOTTISH SKIES

High in the misty Highlands, out by the purple islands
Brave are the hearts that beat beneath Scottish skies.
Wild are the winds to meet you, staunch are the friends
    that greet you,
Kind as the love that shines from fair maidens' eyes.

Scotland the Brave
Clifford Hanley

The Ring of Brodgar, Orkney. A ring of standing stones, shrouded in the mists of time - a monument from the Beaker People.

A FAR OFF SUNLIT PLACE

1

CAITHNESS

As I, all my traceable ancestors and probably many generations before them, were born in the county of Caithness, Scotland, it seems appropriate that my story should start there.

Caithness occupies the north east tip of Scotland, the Ultima Thule of the Scottish mainland (*Maps 1, 2*). If you lay your left hand palm down on a table with thumb and little finger abducted widely, a good idea of the layout of north-east Scotland can be obtained. Caithness would extend from just above the knuckle bone of the index finger up to the tip of that finger then across the tip of the middle finger to the tip of the ring finger, with above these fingers the Pentland Firth and the Atlantic Ocean. The southern border of the county extends from the second joint of the ring finger across the second joint of the middle finger back to the knuckle joint of the index finger, marching to the west and south with the county of Sutherlandshire. In the web of the hand between index finger and abducted thumb lies Inverness, with the Moray Firth bordering the thumb and extending up the index finger as the Caithness coast and outwards and eastwards into the North Sea, while round the tip of the thumb is Aberdeen.

On the east coast the grey waters of the North Sea surge against the equally grey cliffs of the county, cliffs which rise two

3

MAP 1: SCOTLAND, INCLUDING ITS ISLANDS

hundred to four hundred feet sheer from the sea, while the Atlantic Ocean washes its northern shores. Separating the North Sea from the Atlantic and separating Caithness from the Orkney Islands is the Pentland Firth, a notorious stretch of water and particularly treacherous when a swell coming from one direction is opposed to the tide coming from the other.

Caithness is remote from the rest of Britain. Wick, the principal town, for example, is some five hundred miles from London, but only three to three hundred and fifty miles from the Norwegian cities of Stavanger and Bergen. In the past, this remoteness from the rest of Scotland was increased by two natural barriers. The southern border of the county is protected by the Ord of Caithness, a desolate stretch of moor and peat bogs which extends from the high cliffs of the coast in the east to the mountains of Sutherlandshire in the north-west, backed up by Scaraben (2,054 feet), Maiden Pap (1,507 feet), and Morven (2,313 feet), running east to west just south of the Berriedale River.

Further south there is the barrier of the Grampian Mountains stretching across Scotland from above Glasgow in the west to Aberdeenshire in the east. This range of mountains, the Highland Line, divides Scotland into the Highlands to the north and west and the Lowlands to the south and east. For many years the Grampians proved a formidable barrier to travel, to commerce by land within Scotland — and to invasion. When the rest of Britain was a Roman Province, the Pax Romana did not extend north or west of the Grampians. The Highlands remained unconquered.

Whereas Sutherlandshire is a typical Highland county, Caithness is flat and has been described as, 'the Lowlands beyond the Highlands'. The north and east of the county is arable land but a few miles inland the 'endless moor' of author Neil Gunn (born in Caithness) begins. Apart from being an out-run for cattle and sheep, the shielings of the summer months where the animals were herded by the children of the house, the moor was a source of fuel, peat.

Peat is derived from plant and tree remains which have been prevented from decaying in the usual way by the presence of excess moisture at the surface of the soil which excludes the oxygen required by bacteria acting on vegetable matter. After the passage of

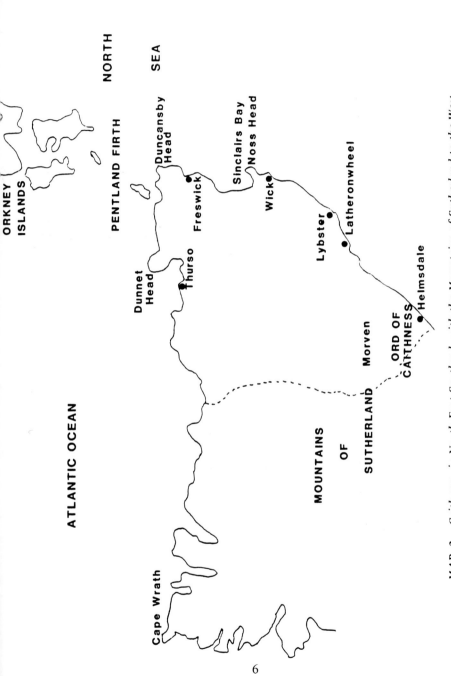

MAP 2: *Caithness, in North East Scotland, with the Mountains of Sutherland to the West.*

ten to twenty thousand years, the vegetable material becomes compressed into the dark, almost solid, deposit of peat.

Each year peat would be cut into divots from peat banks in the moor, set on edge to dry and after some months taken to the crofts where the peat was built into stacks which kept it dry in the winter months. Peat fires were an efficient and economical source of fuel for cooking and heating, giving off a rather acrid pungent blue smoke. In many crofts the fire was never allowed to go out. In the evening it would be 'smoored' to ensure slow combustion and in the morning the peats would be separated and set on end to obtain a funnel effect and allow air to reach the heart of the fire.

The moor is also the home of grouse, hare and red deer and, in remote regions, the wildcat. This animal is not a domestic cat 'gone wild', but a separate species, bigger and heavier, and sporting a blunt ended tail. Even when captured as a kitten and raised in captivity, the wildcat remains untameable and in its natural state is a savage killer. The wildcat is the crest of the Clan Sutherland, coupled with the motto, *Touch not the cat bot a gluv*, or the Latinised, *Sans Peur* (without fear).

The moors are studded with lochs criss-crossed with burns abounding in small trout, while salmon, the only 'fish' of the sporting fisherman, ascend the Thurso, Wick, Dunbeath and Helmsdale rivers to fulfill their destiny.

Agriculture and fishing have been the principal industries of the county. In the past, Caithness paving stones were exported throughout Europe and, since World War II, Caithness glass has gained an excellent reputation. A fine malt whisky ('Old Pultney') is distilled in Wick and is widely used in blending, as well as being available as a single malt.

Lying between latitudes 58°N and 59°N, Caithness is a cool county, the mean summer (July) temperatures being only 12.9°C. On the Continent of Europe such low summer temperatures occur only within the Arctic Circle, and this is reflected in the mean annual surface seawater temperature of 7°C–10°C. As a result, although Caithnessians are a race of seamen and fishermen, many are not efficient swimmers.

The county has a relatively low but fairly frequent rainfall and is windy so that in the summer months an easterly wind blowing in from the North Sea may bring with it coastal mists which can persist for days.

Perhaps a rather bleak picture of the county has been painted and, indeed, Caithness is no tropical paradise or 'sunlit place'. However, it can become a fairyland. On a winter's night, clear, cold and frosty, perhaps with some snow lying on the moors and a falling temperature, the aurora borealis may be seen — a fantastic display in the northern sky of dancing streams of light, the 'Northern Lights', apparently ascending into the heavens. The scientific explanation is that atomic hydrogen emitted from the sun, broken up into protons and electrons, travels to earth and, being electrically charged, is deflected by the earth's magnetic field to high latitudes where it causes a luminescence in the atmosphere at the poles — the aurora borealis in the northern hemisphere, the aurora australis in the southern. So much for science, but folklore and the name, 'the heavenly dancers' is more appealing.

Ancestors

The man lay on the cliff propped on an elbow facing south-west where the setting sun was descending towards Morven. Below him the sea obsessively washed the pebbles of the beach and, reclining thus, he was reminded that just such a scene had been vividly painted in the poetic prose of Maurice Walsh, the Irish novelist with an affection for Scotland. At his descriptive best, Mr Walsh, wrote:

> *Morven with its Pap to the mouth of the sky ... The gold ball of the sun lipped the breast of Morven and lingered in that kiss as well he might.*

Caithness

The Cliffs at Latheronwheel, Caithness, Scotland.
Here once a man 'lay on the cliff ... facing south-west where the setting sun
descended ... the sea obsessively washing the pebbles of the beach ... '

The man fell into a reverie, perhaps he dozed. In his mind he heard the keel of a long boat with dragon headed prow and square sail grating on the shingle of the beach below him and his mind's eye saw helmeted men with blue eyes and fair beards carrying swords, spears and axes wade ashore to be met in bitter conflict by a smaller breed of dark haired men who sprang from the heather and from along the banks of the burn where it met the sea.

Later, looking out to sea he could discern the dim outline of a Spanish galleon running north before the wind and the vengeance of Effingham and Drake, and still later he heard a lone piper and the tramp of Campbell feet on their way from Loch Awe to Wick ...

On wakening, he looked inland to the moor and once again in the twilight the sense of desolation of crofts destroyed in 'the clearances' sweep over him, to be replaced by a feeling of satisfaction that from bays, similar to the one he was standing above, all along the coast fishing boats emerged to harvest the 'Silver Darlings' of Neil Gunn, and to establish the herring industry which was to revolutionise the economy of the county and the financial status of its people.

Mr Maurice Walsh describes my ancestors in this way —

> *Caithness, land of brawn and brain — a dreich treeless land with a desperate bad coast and sailor-men to dare the devil — as hardy a breed of fishermen and deep sea men as ever tailed on a rope.*
>
> *Them Caithness men were regular Kilkenny cats; a mixed breed, Norse and Gael and the two bloods did not mix well. You can see the line of cleavage to this very day. Up about Lybster, you'll find big, fair, stocky lads, and down Dunbeath way, tall, lean black devils.*

The beach at Latheronwheel, Caithness, Scotland.

This is how it occurred: about 5 000 BC there was a movement of people from Thrace, now part of Greece, and from France and Spain to Ireland, Scotland and Wales. These people were the Cruitne or Celtic people. The Romans subsequently misspelled Cruitne, substituting a 'B' for a 'C' and called the people Bruitne, Britons, the Isles of Britain.

These Celts after crossing the Channel in dug-outs probably encountered only a few hundred nomad hunters who had much earlier crossed the strip of land which had previously joined Britain to the continent of Europe, and had no difficulty in penetrating northwards and to the west.

By comparison with the nomad hunters, the Celts were much more civilised, cultivating barley and wheat and breeding pigs, cattle and sheep. They were the builders of chambered tombs. The remains of some sixty of these are to be found in Caithness. Later immigrants were the 'Beaker people', so named because of their characteristic beaker type pottery. This bronze age race (3000–4000 BC) were the builders of the stone circles, the most famous of which is Stonehenge, but many exist spread throughout the country including ones at Inverness, Caithness and Orkney in the north and the Outer Hebrides in the west. These Celtic races were the 'Painted Men' because of their custom of painting their bodies blue with woad and were the people who inhabited Britain for hundreds of years before the arrival of the Romans.

During the five hundred years before the birth of Christ the Roman Empire gradually took shape and eventually what are now Italy, Spain and France as well as North Africa became Roman Provinces. In 56 BC Julius Caesar was campaigning in Gaul and, in his advance up the Breton Peninsula, encountered strong resistance from the Veneti, a powerful sea-faring tribe, who were, however, defeated by an alliance of the Romans and two tribes living on the Bay of Biscay, the Pictones and the Santini. Following this victory the Pictones, a Celtic tribe, became increasingly powerful and spread by sea to Ireland, the Hebrides and around the north of Scotland to Shetland, Orkney, Caithness, Sutherland, Ross and Cromarty. The Pictones settled in these areas, often at the expense of the earlier Celtic tribes. A characteristic feature of their settlement was the

A Stone-Age but of the Skara Brae settlement, Orkney, Scotland.

construction of forts, called duns or brochs. Of the five hundred or so brochs discovered, some one hundred are in Caithness. In Scotland, the Pictones became known as the Picts; they were a short dark race and their language was a form of Gaelic.

Another consequence of the defeat of the Veneti, by the Roman-Santini-Pictone alliance, was that it led to Roman forces crossing the Channel in 55 BC, and again in 54 BC, although after each incursion the legions returned to the Continent and almost one hundred years were to elapse before the Emperor Claudius, in 43 AD, launched a full-scale invasion of the British Isles. This campaign proceeded slowly but, by 80 AD, the Roman forces had penetrated up the east coast to Aberdeenshire. The advance of the Roman forces under Agricola was blocked by the range of mountains we now know as the Grampians. However, Agricola brought the tribes to battle at Mons Graupius (subsequently misspelled Grampius – hence Grampians). The exact site of this battle remains unknown but it was probably fought in the Perth-Dunkeld region, at the foot of 'the great hills'. History, through the son-in-law of Agricola, Tacitus, proclaimed it a great Roman victory against an enemy they called Caledonians. However, despite this claim, the Roman forces retired further south leaving a small line of forts to garrison the area. Over the following twenty to thirty years they increasingly fell back on the line Tyne and Solway, eventually, in 122 AD, constructing a rampart, Hadrian's Wall, a causeway of stone forts and signal towers seventy-five miles long, extending across the country from the Tyne in the east to the Solway in the west. So constant, however, was the pressure from the north on Hadrian's Wall, that twenty years later a forward defensive position was created, the Antonine Wall, extending across the thirty-seven miles of the waist of Scotland, from the Clyde to the Forth. South of Hadrian's Wall, the Pax Romana and the Roman way of life flourished whereas north of the Antonine Wall, in the Highlands and in Caithness, Pictish life and customs prevailed.

Over the ensuing years the Roman garrisons in Britain were steadily reduced to meet increasing pressure on the Empire's frontiers in Europe and, by 400 AD, the Roman occupation of Britain had ended. This left a power vacuum in southern Britain which resulted in a drift south of the northern Picts. Descendants of the Pictones, with a sprinkling of the earlier Cruitne, both Celtic stock, are 'the gaels' of Maurice Walsh, and the depletion of the population in the north by the drift south set the scene for the next act.

In 790 AD, the slender square sailed longships of the Vikings appeared off the British coast, heralding the beginning of the Viking Age, which was to last until 1066. The Vikings or Norsemen came from what is now Norway, Sweden, Denmark and the other Baltic states. In appearance they were fair with ash blonde or gold-blonde hair and blue or grey eyes. Some were tall with long limbs and a high narrow nose: others had more rounded heads with thick-set bodies and had a nasal profile which tended to be concave. They were a brave, adventuresome race. In the eighth Century AD, and for the following three centuries, there was a remarkable expansion of these northern Europeans. As Magnus Magnusson put it in his book *Vikings* —

> ... *they criss-crossed half the world in their open boats and vastly extended its known boundaries ... they voyaged further north and west than any European had ever done before, founding new and lasting colonies ... discovering, exploring and making settlements ... even in North America. They penetrated the depths of Russia founding city states ... pioneering new trade routes along formidable rivers like the Volga and Dnieper, opening up the route to Asia ... They went everywhere there was to go, they dared everything there was to dare ... !*

And this included buccaneering on a scale never hitherto imagined. This expansion and the exploits of the Vikings was made possible by the evolution to the stage of perfection of the longship. Sir Winston Churchill describes it as —

> *This superb instrument of seapower ...*

and pays tribute to —

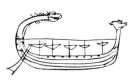

> *... the discipline, the fortitude, the comradeship and martial virtues ...*

of the men who manned these ships.

By the ninth Century AD, Norsemen had settled in Orkney and Shetland, and had crossed the 'Narrow water of the Picts', the Pictland, now Pentland, Firth. Shetland and Orkney became entirely Nordic in language and customs: Sutherlandshire remained largely Pictish; Caithness became a meeting ground of Pictish (Celtic), and Viking (Nordic) cultures, Thus, Maurice Walsh's –

> *A mixed breed, Norse and Gael ...*

The name Caithness itself reflects a mixture of the two cultures, being derived from Cat's Ness. Cat was the son of a Pictish king and 'Ness' the Norse for headland. Place names throughout the county reflect its dual racial nature. Nordic suffixes such as '–ster', a farm (Lybster), and '–wick', a bay (Freswick) abound, while equally common are place names of gaelic (Pictish) origin such as Latheron (place of seals) and Dunbeath (hill of the birch trees). The clan names further reflect this ethnic duality, Sinclairs and Gunns being of Nordic extraction, the Sutherlands and MacKays of Pictish stock.

The earlier allusion to the Spanish Armada in 'the man's' reverie is not unmeant. In 1588, a Spanish fleet of 130 ships under the command of the Duke of Medina Sidonia sailed from Lisbon to pick up an army at Dunkirk, with the intention of invading Queen Elizabeth's England, and re-establishing Roman Catholicism. A running fight ensued in the English Channel in which the Spanish Armada was routed by the 102 smaller ships of Admiral Lord Howard of Effingham and his Vice-Admiral, Sir Francis Drake. Unfortunately for the Spanish the weather deteriorated to such an extent that there could be no turning back. The surviving Spanish ships, driven before the storm, had to flee up the east coast of the British Isles in an attempt to round Orkney and make for Spain down the west coast of the Outer Hebrides and Ireland. In the process more ships were lost, driven ashore on inhospitable coasts including the grey cliffs of Caithness, so that of the original fleet sixty-four galleons and at least 10,000 men were lost. Some of these men, the crews of the ships driven ashore, survived the sea and the local inhabitants and, merging later with them, became the forebears of some of the tall, dark people encountered in pockets on the east coast of Caithness, the Outer Hebrides and Ireland.

The lone piper heard by 'the man' in his reverie played the music his men marched to as Campbell of Glen Orchy led a punitive expedition into Caithness. It happened this way:

The Sixth Earl of Caithness, having fallen on hard times, was forced to sell his Caithness estates to Campbell of Glen Orchy. On the death of the Earl, Campbell, by virtue of this financial transaction, sought to assume the title of Earl of Caithness. This was bitterly resented by the Caithness clans, in particular the Sinclairs, who proceeded to make life as difficult as possible for Glen Orchy. To teach the Sinclairs a lesson, Glen Orchy marched with seven hundred Campbell clansmen from Argyll to Caithness and in 1680, at Altimarloch, some two to three miles from Wick, he inflicted a disastrous defeat on the Sinclairs. Aside from an influx of Campbells who took over the property of the vanquished Sinclairs and who subsequently 'bred like rabbits and spread like bracken', some matters of interest occurred. On the way to Caithness, Glen Orchy's piper composed the famous pipe music of *The Campbells are coming* and, before the battle of Altimarloch, Glen Orchy made in his native gaelic a stirring speech which must rank with some of the greatest pre-conflict exhortations in history. Translated, what he said was —

> *Kinsmen, we are this day in an enemy's country. He that stands by me this day I will stand by him, my son by his son and my grandson by his grandson; and be ye remembering that if this day goes against us, lucky will be the man who ever wins home, for far is the cry to Loch Awe* and far are we from the help of Cruachan.* Fall on!*

Footnote: Loch Awe, a loch in Argyll: Cruachan, a mountain in Argyll, and the Campbell war-cry.

The battle of Altimarloch was the last clan battle to be fought in Scotland.

The infamous Highland Clearances were a direct consequence of the Battle of Culloden and Prince Charles Edward Stuart's defeat by the Duke of Cumberland. Caithness clans took no part in the 1745 rebellion and were therefore spared many of the reprisals which followed. However, they were not spared the effects of legislation which brought the clan system to an end.

The clan system was a tribal system in which each small community had a headman or laird who, in turn, gave allegiance to the Chief, who was a father figure. Thus, The Sutherland, The MacKay or The MacLeod was the head of the clan and to him all Sutherlands, MacKays or MacLeods gave their allegiance. In turn, he was loyal to his clansmen, looking after their interests and ensuring their protection. One of the most important effects of the post-Culloden legislation was to deprive the clans of their Chiefs and the Chiefs of their lands. The newcomers who took over these lands were simply the landowners; they commanded no loyalty from the broken clans and gave none.

The second factor of importance in causing the Clearance was the demand for soldiers, and for uniforms to clothe them, brought about by the wars Britain had fought against France, the campaigns in India, the American War of Independence, and the Napoleonic campaigns. Wool was therefore valuable and the new Highland landowners quickly appreciated that woolly Cheviot sheep were more profitable than penurious tenants. To replace the latter with the former, crofting communities were forcibly evicted, their crofts burned and their land turned over to sheep. Some of the dispossessed crofters joined the army but many emigrated to Canada, America, New Zealand and Australia. The Highlands, the glens and the moors became depopulated. One can still to this day see the gable end of a ravaged croft, heather encroaching on a grassy patch that was once a tilled field, or the crumbling wall of a small kitchen garden scattered throughout the Highlands. Robert Louis Stevenson had such scenes in his mind when he wrote —

A Far Off Sunlit Place

Grey recumbent tombs of the dead in desert places,
Standing stones on the vacant wine-red moor,
Hills of sheep, and the homes of the silent vanished races
And winds austere and pure:
Be it granted to behold you again in dying
Hills of home! and hear again the call,
Hear about the graves of the martyrs the pewees crying
And hear no more at all.

In Caithness, the Clearances were less extensive than in Sutherlandshire and elsewhere in the Highlands and the abundant fishing around the coast mitigated hardship and hunger. Indeed, in the latter years of the 18th Century and in the 19th Century fishing, particularly herring fishing, was to become a major industry and 'The silver darlings' of author Neil Gunn were to do much to improve the mediaeval way of life of the Caithness crofter.

The sea wall and harbour at Latheronwheel, Caithness — a typical small harbour
to guard the herring fishing boats, and those who sailed in them.

THE FAMILY

My known family history starts in the eventful Eighteenth Century.

In 1702, Anne, daughter of the deposed James II, became Queen of England and Scotland, and reigned until her death in 1714. Although her reign was short she was to see her general, the Duke of Marlborough, emerge as one of the 'Great Captains of War' with ten years of unbroken victories against the might of Louis XIV of France, including the battles of Blenheim (1704), Ramilles (1706), Oudenarde (1708) and Malplaquet (1709) to his credit. In the subsequent Treaty of Utrecht (1713), in which Britain gained Gibraltar, Minorca, Nova Scotia and Newfoundland, the foundations of the first British Empire were laid. Queen Anne's reign was also notable for poets such as Alexander Pope (1688-1744), for writers like Jonathan Swift (1667-1745), for architects (Christopher Wren, 1632-1723), and for advances in science (Isaac Newton, 1642-1727) while, politically, the Union of the Parliaments of Scotland and England was achieved in 1707.

On Anne's death the Elector of Hanover, a great-grandson of James I, accepted the Government's invitation to the throne and became George I of England and Scotland. James II, who had been obliged to flee the country in 1688, made an abortive attempt in 1715 to restore the House of Stuart to the throne and Roman

Catholicism to the country but otherwise the transition was accomplished smoothly, largely due to Robert Walpole, the Prime Minister.

George II succeeded his father in 1727 and was to reign until 1760. During these years William Pitt, later Earl of Chatham and one of Britain's most outstanding Prime Ministers, ably served by men such as Generals Wolfe and Amherst in Canada, Clive in India, and Admirals Boscawen and Hawke in the West Indies, was to establish firmly the first British Empire including a British America which stretched from Montreal to New Orleans.

In 1760 George III became King. The American War of Independence was to follow (1775-83), and the previous years of victory were now followed by years of defeat, partly due to George III's intransient nature and partly brought about by a French, Spanish and Dutch alliance with the Americans. The Treaty of Versailles (1783) sought to dismember the first British Empire but in the same year William Pitt 'the younger' (son of the Earl of Chatham) became Prime Minister. He was to preside over establishing Britain's second Empire, an Empire which was to include Canada, India, Australia and New Zealand.

In the meantime, in 1789, the French Revolution sent tremors through the civilised world and flowing from it came the Napoleonic era which was to persist into the next century until ended by the battle of Waterloo (1815).

So much for the momentous happenings of the 18th Century, but events which have a more direct bearing on this story commenced in 1741, when George II persuaded Parliament to engage in a European war, the war of the Austrian Succession on the side of the Dutch and Austrians against Frederick (later 'the Great') of Prussia, France and Spain. In 1743 King George and his younger son the Duke of Cumberland defeated French forces in the Battle of Dettingen, the last occasion in which a British king fought in person at the head of his soldiers, but in 1745 Cumberland was defeated by the French Marshal Saxe at Fontenoy.

Possibly because this campaign had drained troops from Britain to fight in Flanders, Prince Charles Edward Stuart (the 'Young Pretender', 'Bonnie Prince Charlie') took the opportunity to land on the west coast of Scotland. In this he was given moral support, but no troops, by the French because of the diversory value of the move. Despite the advice of his local Highland chiefs, Prince Charlie raised his standard on 19th August, 1745, at Glenfinnan at the head of Loch Shiel. At first all went well. The Prince occupied Edinburgh, defeated the forces of Lieutenant-Colonel Sir John Cope at Prestonpans, a small coastal town some nine miles south-east of Edinburgh, and advanced into England as far as Derby some one hundred and fifty miles from London. There was panic in the capital. The Duke of Cumberland and many of his regiments were recalled from Flanders. However, it had become apparent to the Prince and his advisers that there was little popular support for his cause or his religion and the Highland Army withdrew back into Scotland.

Eventually, on April 16th, 1746, an exhausted Highland force of now barely 5,000 men faced the Duke of Cumberland's highly professional army, numbering some 9,000 across Culloden Moor, on the outskirts of Inverness. In the ensuing battle the Highlanders were routed. The Prince escaped, but in the battle and pursuit between six and twelve hundred of his men were killed. Cumberland is said to have shown no mercy after the battle and this and the subsequent 'pacification' of the Highlands earned him his title of 'Butcher'. Certainly throughout the Highlands glen after glen was laid waste, 'the men shot or hung, the women raped, houses and buildings burned. What was said of the Romans some seven hundred years earlier, 'They make a desert and they call it peace' could equally be said of the Hanoverians.

Some five years after the Battle of Culloden, and one hundred and fifteen miles to the north, four of my ancestors, the earliest I have been able to trace, were born. Unfortunately, my great-great-great-grandparents' birth dates could not be traced but it is known that Robert Sutherland married a Catherine Miller and their son, Peter, was born in 1776, while on my mother's side of the family, William Bremner married Jane Irvine and their son Andrew was born in 1771. Assuming that the parents of Peter Sutherland and Andrew Bremner were in their twenties when they married, but not knowing the places they occupied in their respective sibships, they would probably have been born between 1750 and 1755 (*Table 1*).

RELATIONSHIP TO JMS

RELATIONSHIP TO JMS	PATERNAL FAMILY —SUTHERLAND—	MATERNAL FAMILY —BREMNER—
Great-great-great grandparents	Robert (c.1750- ?) *m* Catherine Millar	William (c.1750-) *m* Jane Irvine
Great-great grandparents	Peter (1776–1859) *m* Elizabeth Paterson	Andrew (1774–1862) *m* Elizabeth Morrison (1772–1874)
Great grandparents	Peter (1815–1897) *m* Catherine Sutherland (1817–1888)	Simon (1820–1900) *m* Helen Alexander (1848–1878)
Grandparents	Peter (1854–1887) *m* Janet Bruce (1852–1944)	John (1857- ?) *m* Catherine Manson (1860- ?)
Parents	Donald (1887–1944)	Kathleen (1887–1920)
	JMS (1919-) *m* Patricia Campbell (1920-)	
Children	Donald McKee (1945-) *m* Gillian (1946-)	Iain (1951–1973)
Grandchildren	Jennifer (1972-) Louise (1974-)	

Table 1: THE KINDRED OF JOHN MacKAY SUTHERLAND – HIS ANCESTORS AND SUCCESSORS

22

Thus Robert and Catherine Sutherland, William and Jane Bremner, grew up, married and raised their families during the subjugation of the Highlands in the aftermath of the '45 rebellion. However, as crofter-fisherman families in Caithness, it is doubtful if their lives were changed greatly. They lost their chiefs, and were forbidden to speak gaelic; they were forbidden to wear tartan but normally their woollen garments had no design, they were also forbidden to carry a sword but normally no weapon would be carried while fishing or working the croft — and the sword would be quite safe hidden in the thatch of the croft. In the 1750s and for several subsequent decades their hard, primitive lifestyle probably continued with little change.

The few military roads in Caithness were a series of pot holes and the other roads merely tracks winding through the heather. One hundred years were to pass before a railway line traversed the county and a similar time before telegraphic communication with the south was established. Certainly, the parents of Robert Sutherland and Catherine Millar and those of William Bremner and Jane Irvine, and probably the young couples themselves after their respective marriages, would have lived in a windowless house with the smoke from the peat fire escaping from a hole in the roof placed to one side of the fireplace to avoid rain putting the fire out in wet weather. The sleeping quarters would be to one side of this room and on the other side, separated by a partition, accommodation for the animals. Their food, served on flat stones or in wooden dishes, would consist of oatmeal cooked in various ways, milk, cheese, an occasional egg, cabbage, fish (fresh and dried) and only rarely mutton or pork. The croft itself would comprise a few acres, a small flock of sheep, some cattle and pigs, a cow or two and a garron (native) horse. Grain would be the principal crop and some vegetables would be grown in a small kitchen garden. There would also be an outrun of moor where animals would be herded by the children or tethered in the summer months.

Two events occurred which were to allow the Sutherlands and the Bremners to emerge from the middle ages. Between 1754 and 1767, potatoes were introduced and the herring-fishing industry became established. Potatoes and herring became the staple diet in

A crofter's bome, Orkney. Cliff-top ruins of a typical croft dating from tbe early Nineteentb Century.

the county for more than a century and the herring industry was to augment greatly the economy of the crofting community and with it their housing and living standards. It remained, however, a life of hard work for crofter-fishermen and their families during the last years of the 18th Century, and through the 19th. In the summer months Peter Sutherland (1776-1859), Andrew Bremner (1774-1862), Peter Sutherland (1815-1897), and Simon Bremner (1820-1900) — *Table 1*, would exchange the croft for the sea and might even extend the fishing season and augment their income by joining a southern boat for a time fishing, for example, out of Yarmouth. On returning to Caithness the work of the croft, with the assistance of wife and family, would continue. The peats which had been drying on the moor would be taken home and stacked alongside the croft; the grain crop would be scythed and later the land ploughed, seed sown, potatoes planted, the lambing supervised, the peats cut and set to dry — and another fishing season.

However, the hard working life lead on to my great-grand parents (Peter Sutherland, 1815-97 — Catherine Sutherland, 1817-88: Simon Bremner, 1820-1900 — Helen Alexander, 1830-78) enjoying greatly improved living conditions. Now the typical house was a stone cottage with a thatched roof, windows, a chimney or two and flagstoned floors covered in 'the room' by a rug or a sheep-skin or two. This was the 'but and ben' with a closet typical of rural Scotland. The 'but' end of the cottage was the kitchen with a fireplace, chairs, table, a kist of oatmeal and a barrel of salted herring. Boxbeds built back to back separated the kitchen from the 'closet'. The 'ben' end of the house would also have a bed, a table, chairs and a fireplace. The byre and stable might well be attached to one end of the house in the fashion of 'the long house' of Nordic origin, but now it would have a separate door and a wall would separate it from the dwelling while in some crofts the byre and stable would be separate from the house, being situated either at right angles to it or behind it.

My family is a mixture of Celtic and Nordic strains. The Sutherlands are a Highland clan and my ancestors infiltrated Caithness from Sutherlandshire, settling in the southern parish of Latheron and living the lives of crofter-fishermen up to the and

25

including my grandparents, Peter Sutherland (1854–87) and Janet Bruce (1852–1944). Peter was lost at sea in 1887, aged thirty-three years, leaving his widow to bring up six young children. Janet, his widow, and my paternal grandmother, did this so successfully that fifteen years later an article in the local newspaper, *The John O'Groat Journal* of 10th February, 1922, reads —

Mrs Sutherland was early left a widow ... she had a hard struggle to bring them [the six children] *up; but with the characteristic grit and affection of Scottish mothers of the best type, she devoted her life to their welfare, ever culcating the highest principles of character and conduct.*

The same newspaper article goes on —

Although the Sutherland children started their adult lives at the lowest rung of the ladder their background and upbringing paid dividends.

Peter, the eldest, became a very successful businessman in Glasgow, and Alec, a farmer and noted stockbreeder in Caithness. John, killed in World War I, was according to his obituary, 'one of the most expert craftsmen both as a tailor and cutter in the North'. Kate married a school teacher destined to become headmaster of a large Glasgow school, while Elizabeth married a sheep farmer and contractor in Argyll. Donald, my father, became Laird of Reisgill, Lybster and Swiney estates, a successful farmer and an hotel proprietor.

My father was born on 10th March, 1887, some five months before his father lost his life. However, after working on the croft, then as a footman to Admiral Sinclair at Dunbeath Castle, and as a secretary to Mr Donald Mackay, a judge of the Land Court, he and his brother, John, in partnership purchased a general store and  tailoring business at Latheronwheel in 1912. August 1914, saw the outbreak of World War I and John, a good shot, an expert horseman and a peace time member of the Lovat Scouts, was immediately mobilised. He served on the Western Front with the Lovat Scouts, and later with the Gordon Highlanders as a corporal and a sniper until killed in August, 1918, shortly before the War ended, by a sniper's bullet from the opposite side.

My grandmother, Janet Sutherland, née Bruce, lived to be a very old lady and an inscription on a gravestone in Latheron Old Burial Ground reads —

PETER SUTHERLAND, FORSE DIED 25-8-1887
Aged 33

HIS WIFE, JANET BRUCE, DIED AT LYBSTER 1-6-1944
Aged 92.

Janet does not, however, hold the family record for longevity as Elizabeth Morrison, widow of Alexander Bremner who lived to be eighty-eight years, died in 1874, aged 101.

The Bremners, the maternal side of my parentage, unlike the Sutherlands, are of Nordic extraction and lived in the parish of Canisbay in the Freswick—John O'Groats area. I recall my grandfather John Bremner as being a veritable Viking, tall, strongly built, greyhaired when I knew him, and with piercing blue eyes. How the Bremners came to Caithness is uncertain. It is probable that John Bremner's ancestors crewed a longship and like many of their compatriots who colonised Shetland, Orkney and the north-east of Scotland, they settled in Caithness.

There is an alternative theory that the Bremners may be of north German extraction. The story goes ...... Bremerhaven, near Bremen, has been for many years a port of north Germany, and in the distant past a ship from that port joined the numerous vessels wrecked off the treacherous north-east Caithness coast. The survivors who made the shore and safety did not speak English or Gaelic but in the way of seamen and perhaps by their ship's papers were able to indicate that they came from Bremen. The locals came to refer to them as 'the Bremeners' in the same way as we might refer to 'Southerners'. Perhaps because returning to Germany from the north of Scotland was difficult in those days, or for other reasons, some of

The Pentland Firth and Marwick Head, Orkney. The cliff-top monument is to the memory of Lord Kitchener and Ship's Company, HMS Hampshire (sunk in 1916).

the Bremeners settled in Caithness, in time marrying Caithness girls. Because German surnames may have been difficult for the locals to pronounce, their descriptive name was retained and adopted as a surname, being shortened in the course of time from Bremener to Bremner.

Like the Sutherland side of the family living further south on the east coast of Caithness, the Bremners were crofter-fishermen, although the deep sea instinct was present in great-great-great-grandfather William Bremner, great-great-grandfather Andrew and great-grandfather Simon who were, in addition, Pentland Firth pilots. In the 18th and 19th Centuries there was a considerable volume of trade between northern Europe and America and ships carrying commerce to and from the Americas frequently gained the Atlantic or the North Sea by passing through the Pentland Firth. In the days of sailing ships the Pentland Firth was difficult to navigate and to ensure a safe passage pilots were engaged, ships coming from the west signalling for a pilot before reaching Dunnet Head, while ships coming from Europe would take on a pilot off Noss Head at the southern end of Sinclairs' Bay. There Andrew Bremner, for example, would be rowed out in his boat with a two man crew to the sailing ship. After taking the ship through the Pentland Firth he would be landed at Thurso by ship's boat to start on a twenty to twenty-five mile walk back to his croft at Freswick. Sometimes the pilot's boat would be taken in tow and the pilot and his crew would sail back to Sinclairs' Bay. Occasionally, if the weather turned very bad, the pilot could not be landed and he would travel to the ship's destination. Piloting was well paid, the fee for taking a boat through the Pentland Firth being three guineas with, in addition, fringe benefits of duty free tobacco and alcohol and salted meat.

Despite this hard and often hazardous life, Andrew Bremner died in 1862 aged eighty-eight years and his son Simon was drowned while fishing in Freswick Bay in 1900 at the age of eighty. Although the Pentland Firth remains stormy and treacherous, the advent of steamships greatly lessened its hazards and the need for Pentland Firth pilots disappeared into history.

John and Catherine Bremner, my maternal grandparents, farmed a croft at Freswick and John was also a fisherman. Their

Nurse Kathleen Bremner, mother of
John MacKay Sutherland.

eldest daughter, born in 1887, was Kathleen Barrie Bremner, my mother. Her two sisters never married, possibly due to World War I virtually wiping out a generation of young men. One brother qualified in medicine, becoming in due course medical officer of health for Sutherlandshire, and another brother became a farmer.

Kathleen was made of adventuresome stuff. In an age when few Caithnessians left the county, unless they had enlisted in the navy or army, and even fewer Caithness women, Miss Bremner took herself off to the Royal Infirmary, Dumfries, where she achieved 'A General Nursing Diploma with Honours'. After nursing for a time in Edinburgh, she took her Midwifery Diploma at Newcastle-upon-Tyne and in 1913 returned to Caithness as District Nurse, Latheron Nursing Association. It was at Latheronwheel she met Donald Henry Sutherland, merchant, my father-to-be. If we may glance at Kathy's diary we would see this entry —

Dec. 24, 1915. Walked home. Dan proposed.
Considering matters.

Nurse Kathleen Bremner gave 'the matter' fairly lengthy consideration because it was not until March, 1917, that she and Dan were married.

On August 20th, 1919, I was born and it is probable that this event gave considerable pleasure to at least three people; to me because I had been rather confined for the previous nine months, and to my parents, Kathleen and Dan Sutherland, because I was their

firstborn. I was 'at home' in the house adjacent to the shop, and as I was being delivered into this world the lintel of a store which was being built beside the shop was 'placed into position'. My proud father was so hospitable to the workmen on the site that a half-day's work was lost subsequent to my arrival. In later years when passing through Latheronwheel — *en route* to clinics at Thurso and Wick — I always saluted the store, situated on the right hand side of the road, as I passed heading north, as one would an old friend, a contemporary.

Kathleen Sutherland, née Bremner, with son John Sutherland in arms. Photo 1920.

Unfortunately, I never got to know Kathy as in December, 1920, she died from an ectopic pregnancy. Her obituary describes her, however, as having —

> *A bright and lovable disposition ... a favourite with all ... richly endowed with qualities fitted for the profession she loved so well.*

and a family friend regarded her as 'a radiant woman'.

John Sutherland, aged 10 months, in 1920

Subsequently, I was brought up by my father's eldest brother Peter and his wife Jessie, in Glasgow. They had no children and, although never legally adopted, for practical purposes I became their son with the added bonus of having 'a second father' in Caithness. I lived most of the year in Glasgow, going to school and eventually to University in that city, but spent the long summer vacation with Dan, my natural father, in Caithness at Reisgill farm near Lybster. I had the best of two worlds, my 'parents' in Glasgow and the advantages of a city education, and a supernumerary father in Caithness with whom I spent my vacations, enjoying to the full the freedom of country life.

DONALD HENRY SUTHERLAND
Photo 1937
'an extraordinary able and astute man'.

Donald Henry Sutherland (my father, or 'DH' as he was widely known), according to his solicitor and friend Harold Georgeson,

> *...was an extraordinary able and astute man, as I can testify, and no-one knew him better than I did. I remember old Alec Grant, your faithful servitor* [gamekeeper, on Lybster], *apropos your worthy father, remarking in a whisper, 'the very best friend and a wonderful master, but a terrible enemy!'*

My then Chief, Dr D.K. Adams, had this to say —

> *Your father had all the attributes that makes Scotland respected and esteemed.*

My own recollection is of a dynamic driving force. A clear thinker with an astute brain, he would have made an excellent lawyer. Physically, he was a very broad shouldered man, but due to a riding accident in his youth in which he fractured his spine he was not tall. Perhaps embittered by the death of his brother and partner, John, and by the death of his young wife, I do not recall him having a great sense of humour. He was, however, a wonderful raconteur and could make the short hairs at the back of the head lift with fearful anticipation. This is one of his stories.

> *In the days when I was young the causewaymire was a lonely moorland road running from Latheron across the county towards Thurso. It was, indeed, little more than a boggy track running across the moor and winding round peat bogs and because of a virtual absence of human habitations it was much frequented by highwaymen. Many a murder was committed on the causewaymire and the bodies flung into a peat bog. Peat, however, has a wonderful preserving action so that many years later people cutting peat at the peat banks for fuel would come across bodies with hair and features so well preserved they might have been alive yesterday.*

*One evening when I was a lad of 14 or 15, I was
driving a pony and trap across the causewaymire and as
the dusk deepened a mist spread in from the North Sea
and seemed to come out of the peat bogs themselves.
From time to time a startled curlew would rise from the
grass and heather bordering the road with an eerie,
forlorn cry like a soul in torment. The soft clip-clop
of the pony's hooves was the only other sound but as
we passed dulochs, small boggy lochans filled with black
peaty water and said to be bottomless, I remembered
tales of voices coming from the dulochs inviting a
passer-by to join them. To do so was fatal!*

*With the mist and darkness increasing it was better
to let the pony find its way so I sat holding the reins
with only sufficient pressure on the bit to give the
garron some support if she stumbled in a pot hole when
suddenly every hair on my head and neck prickled
with horror!*

*Coming out of the mist behind the trap I heard
hoarse deep breathing. I tightened the reins and urged
the pony into a trot. The hoarse breathing kept pace
with me. The trot became a canter. Still the menacing
breathing followed and as I glanced over my shoulder
in terror I could see in the mist ghostly horns – the
Devil himself was after me!*

*I was filled with terror but as the garron was tiring
I could only think of pulling off the road and hiding, if
I could, in the heather. I pulled the pony sharply off
the road onto what appeared to be firm ground and as
I glanced fearfully over my shoulder a magnificent
stag with a full set of antlers went bounding by.*

Peter Alexander Sutherland (my 'adoptive' father) was the
oldest member of 'Granny Sutherland's' family and was only thirteen
years old when his father was lost at sea. He worked on the croft and
certainly went to sea in the fishing season as the ship's boy. In later
years he would recall the hardships attached to this work and of his

attempts to prepare a meal for the crew in a small, dimly lit, fo'c's'le reeking of the combined smells of herring, paraffin oil and cooking. Despite this when, as a successful business man in Glasgow, he returned to Caithness on holiday he invariably went out for a night or two on one of the fishing boats still based on Lybster. Peter Sutherland was one of the finest men I have known. Largely self taught and essentially a 'self made man', he had a sense of values, a Highland dignity, loyalty to and pride of family, which made him one of Nature's gentlemen. Like most Highlanders, Peter was not demonstrative but he was, like his wife my Aunt Jessie, tremendously supportive. Both took an interest and pride in my school and university progress. I could not have had better parents.

*Peter Sutherland,
uncle of
John MacKay Sutherland,
in the bows of the fishing boat
'Gleaner', in 1939.*

*'A man with Highland dignity
and one of the finest
men I have known.'*

A FAR OFF SUNLIT PLACE | 3

THE PRE-WAR YEARS, 1920-1939

I was born on August 20th, 1919, the year in which the Peace Treaty with Germany was signed and two months after the German Fleet was scuttled at Scapa Flow, in the Orkney Islands. In 1921, 91 Mossgiel Road, Newlands, Glasgow, became my new home and I was to continue to live there with my Uncle and Aunt, Peter and Jessie Sutherland, my 'parents' by arrangement, throughout my school and University days.

For the average British citizen, the 1920s were a relatively uneventful post-war period punctuated by a general strike in 1926. Indeed, through to 1935, little disturbed the even tenor of our ways. Hindenberg might appoint Adolf Hitler Chancellor of Germany in 1933, and Hitler might make himself dictator within a year but this sort of thing was an idiosyncrasy of the Italians and Germans and, after all, Benito Mussolini had been the Italian dictator since 1922 without any obvious ill effect. The invasion of Abyssinia by Italy (1935-36) however, aroused some anti-fascist sentiments but few of us regarded the Spanish Civil War (1936-39) as what it was — a blooding of the legions of Germany and Italy, a dress rehearsal for the much greater conflict to come. We were probably more disturbed that King Edward VIII, after a reign of only 325 days, should desert Britannia for the favours of an American divorcee. One man was not myopic. Winston Spencer Churchill repeatedly warned the country and the Government of our growing peril and was widely regarded as a war-monger for his pains.

The terrace at Mossgiel Road, Glasgow.
To the left is 'Morven', number 91 Mossgiel Road —
my home during school and university days.

During these years the affairs of Peter and Donald Sutherland prospered. Peter, now a clothing manufacturer, was described in a newspaper of the day as being 'a highly successful businessman in the City' while Dan, my father, became sole proprietor of Reisgill, Lybster and Swiney Estates, farmed Reisgill, and became co-proprietor first of Navidale House Hotel, near Helmsdale, and later of the Station Hotel, Wick.

I was, therefore, brought up in mildly affluent middle class circumstances but, in the Scottish tradition and by comparison with modern standards, fairly strictly — as were all my friends. Certainly, from a financial point of view, I was invariably in reduced circumstances, receiving for pocket money two pence per week at five to six years of age, sixpence to a shilling later in my first decade and two shillings in my second until I was given an allowance of four pounds sterling per month when I went to University. This was the scale of munificence accorded most of my friends and contemporaries and, indeed, it was not unreasonable when ice-cream cost a half-penny to two pence, potato chips cost a penny to two pence, two pence to six pence gained admission to a cinema and six pence entry to a first class football match.

My aunt and uncle being childless, I lacked brothers and sisters but not friends or companions as a considerable number of boys of a similar age (and, eventually, girls!) lived in the neighbourhood – Ian Thomson Gordon Stuart, Rowell Lockhart, Gordon Watson, Alastair Smith, Charles Dunbar, Ian Lyon, Robert McColl, Ian Lambie, Walter Templeton, to name a few. All were to serve in one or other of the Armed Services in a few years time. Some, Gordon Stuart, Rowell Lockhart, Robert McColl, did not survive the War; another, Ian, now Sir John Thomson MBE served with the Fijian military forces against the Japanese in the Solomon Islands, and after becoming Chief Secretary to the Governor of Fiji (second-in-command after the Governor), was appointed Governor of the British Virgin Islands. Following his Caribbean sojourn, and after Fiji's

In the garden at 91 Mossgiel Road, Glasgow. Peter and Jessie Sutherland, with John MacKay Sutherland.

'The Warriors'
Three High School 'men'
of Glasgow.

Left to right:
Major General Charles
Dunbar, CBE;
John Sutherland; and
Sir John Thomson CBE.

Photo, c. 1935

independence in 1970, Ian returned at the personal request of the Fijian Governor to the post of Chairman of the Fiji Sugar Industry and Chairman of 'Air Pacific' before retiring to Argyll, Scotland. Charles Dunbar, a doctor's son, and one time medical student, served with distinction in the Army throughout the War and remained in the Services, achieving in due course the rank of Major-General, and a CBE.

My aunt and uncle (my 'parents') invariably employed a living-in maid in these pre-war years. This had a number of advantages as far as I was concerned. Except on the maid's days off I had no household or domestic duties. However, because of this, and in no way helped by being a hospital resident followed by two years in the Navy, I was a rather undomesticated individual on returning to civilian life as a married man. I soon learned! Secondly, our maids were for the most part young women, so although lacking a sister or brother, there was generally someone of a similar age to myself in the house to chat with. Finally, sitting at the kitchen fire with the young lady in the evening I had my education rounded off by reading *True Romances, The Peoples' Friend, Red Letter Weekly* and similar literary gems while she read my weeklies, *Rover* and *Adventure*, or followed the stirring adventures of *Dixon Hawke* in that series of detective novels.

My friends and I nearly all attended Glasgow High School, and as the school was then situated at Elmbank Street in the centre of the City, and we lived on the southern outskirts, this entailed a journey of some 40 minutes each way by tramcar or train and a considerable walk in either event. The High School had a long tradition, being in direct descent from the Glasgow Grammar School which was founded by Glasgow Cathedral and was in existence prior to 1140. In 1460, control of the school passed to the Councillors of the Borough of Glasgow, who acted as patrons and governors, the Roman Catholic clergy providing Rectors until 1560, and thereafter the Reformed Church.

In his book *The High School of Glasgow* H.A. Ashmall reproduced the School Prospectus for 1838/39, which indicates that —

> *The object of this Institution is to afford, at a moderate expense, a complete Course of Education, qualifying Young Gentlemen for the UNIVERSITIES, for entering the ARMY or NAVY or for engaging in COMMERCIAL PURSUITS.*

In the garden at Mossgiel Road, Glasgow.
Left to right: Peter Sutherland (uncle), Jessie Sutherland (aunt),
and John. 'We three in the garden at Morven, 1937'.

The school authorities adopted a more cautious line in a later prospectus (1903/4), remarking, perhaps somewhat ruefully but at the same time threateningly –

> *Few boys can be made scholars; all boys can be taught to behave like gentlemen.*

The High School was non-denominational. It was a day school only. Although fee paying, because it was subsidised by the City of Glasgow, the fees were considerably less than those of our great local rival, Glasgow Academy, or the prestigious boarding schools of Scotland, such as Strathallan, Glenalmond, Fettes or Merchisons. Although in this way socially inferior, High School was otherwise on a par with the other Great Scottish Schools and in the years before World War II no Scottish International XV took the field without a number of High School FPs in the side, which gives rise to this story.

At the outbreak of the second World War, a former pupil of Glasgow High School and an ex-member of the Officers Training Corps was attending an interview for a commission in the Army:

Interviewing Officer (IO) *– an Englishman, What school?*
Former pupil (FP), *Glasgow High School, Sir.*
IO, *Has anyone of note attended that school?*
FP, *Er, Bonar-Law, Campbell Bannerman* [both Prime Ministers], *Sir John Moore* [of Corunna fame and incidentally the son of a Glasgow doctor], *Lord Clyde* [C. in C. India during the Mutiny] ...
IO [interrupting], *H'm, anyone else?*
FP [with a flash of inspiration], *Why yes, Sir, Wilson Shaw!**
IO, *Good God, man! Why did you not say so in the first instance! Accepted for Officers Training Course!*

Footnote: Wilson Shaw was School Captain during one of my senior years and as an FP was one of the greatest players of rugby football to don a High School and Scotland jersey.

In the 1930s school discipline was strict but not harsh. Prefects were responsible for general discipline such as wearing school uniform and their punishment was restricted to bestowing lines on a culprit. Masters were empowered to enforce classroom discipline with 'the belt' – a leather strap which was applied forcefully by the master to the offender's outstretched hands held one beneath the other. If my recollection is correct, for a punishment in excess of 'two of the best', the pupil had the right of having the punishment witnessed by another master but this was rarely requested as it was generally held that an audience might only spur the master bestowing the punishment to greater efforts. The ultimate penalty was expulsion, carried out only once in my time on a joker caught having a gin and tonic in the clubhouse after a Masters *versus* Boys golf match. For lesser crimes, retribution was meted out by the Head Janitor, Sergeant-Major J.T. Bowes, a redoubtable figure, resplendent in purple frockcoat and top hat, with a fiercely pointed waxed moustache. He was once described by a former pupil as –

A complete man, an unparalled janitor – perhaps the Absolute Janitor!

After a rather slack first few years at High School, I decided to become a farmer. My father, however, insisted that I spend my Christmas vacation working at Reisgill before finally making up my mind. During these few weeks the intensely cold frosty weather, which so stiffened my fingers that I could barely unharness the horses with which I had been working, also withered my husbandry ambition and I decided to improve my scholastic performance. My school masters were at first worried, thinking I was seriously ill and later, after I had landed some prizes at the end of the year, rather smug in the belief that they had achieved a transformation in at least one drone.

In the 1930s class numbers varied from 15 to 30, depending on the subject. The masters were generally respected; some were held in awe; a few were revered. The psychology of teaching may have been in its infancy at that time but High School masters mixed the ingredients of strict discipline, a man to man approach, an obvious desire for their pupils to achieve their goals, and participation in our social occasions in a most successful manner. I am grateful to them.

When I joined the school in 1929, Dr Peter Pinkerton (1914–1930) was Rector. He was a mathematician, and as I knew him, a kindly elderly man. In some ways he was the antithesis of Rector Talman (1931–1950), his successor, who was an educationalist, had taught Constitutional Law at Glasgow University, and believed that at fifteen a pupil should no longer be taught but allowed to learn. Fortunately, most of his masters adhered to the view that 'teaching does help the willing learner', a concept I firmly believe in. It was traditional, although not officially compulsory, to play rugby union and to be a member of the Officers' Training Corps. The Objects of the Corps (1910) furnish a picture of the past:

(1)   Improvement of physique
(2)   Inculcation of habits of obedience, discipline and self control
(3)   A quickened sense of school life, Country, and the development of public spirit
(4)   A realisation of the responsibilities which must be incurred and the duties which must be discharged as Citizens of the Empire.

An historical picture, perhaps, but these duties were fully discharged in two World Wars. In World War II, 1563 former pupils served in the Armed Forces, about one in ten gave their lives. In the holocaust of World War I, nearly 500 ex-pupils were killed on active service.

After finishing homework on long summer evenings and at weekends soccer, cricket and later golf were our principal recreational activities. Largely because the High School's playing fields were at Anniesland on the north-west side of the City, whereas Newlands was on the south side, I, and most of my friends, played soccer rather than rugby union football. Our team, Ashburn, competed in a junior league and Ian Thomson and I, with a number of our friends, played each Saturday morning for that team. Ian and I, in our last year at school, were considerably taken with ourselves when we were invited to play for a more senior club but as I recall my participation ceased after a couple of matches when I tore ligaments and a cartilage in my right knee. I played only one further soccer match. Some five years later I turned out for the Western Infirmary Residents *v* the Porters annual football game. Never has a pitch seemed so long and never muscles and joints so painful! The real problem lay in the fact that I had arranged to meet Pat, then my fiancé, for an evening meal followed by a cinema show. She was horrified when, battered and bruised, I hirpled into the restaurant. Worse was to come: the picture was *Gone with the Wind*, and throughout that unending film the muscles of my legs would go into spasm and to relieve the cramp I would have to vacate my seat and walk to and fro at the back of the cinema. I was not popular with Pat – or with the couples occupying the last row of the back stalls!

On Saturday afternoons during the football season my friends and I would generally watch a senior football match. Third Lanark was our favoured team and Cathkin Park, where they played, our favoured ground partly because Mr Thomson, Ian's father, was a director of the Club and we gained free admission and partly because Third Lanark played in red shirts and white trunks, the same colours as Ashburn's rig, allowing us to identify readily with Third Lanark's 'stars' such as Neil Dewar and Jimmy Carabine who were Scottish internationals. Saturday evenings were pleasantly occupied in one or others' homes playing records or, if funds permitted, paying a visit to a local cinema. As our teenage years progressed golf became a favourite pastime. In addition to playing on our own courses, Cowglen, Whitecraigs, Cathkin Braes, as we grew older my friends and I played on all the famous Ayrshire golf courses, Prestwick, Old Troon, Portland, Glasgow Gailes, Western Gailes, Belleisle, Turnberry and many more.

Gordon Stuart's father was a keen golfer and from time to time, accompanied by a friend, he would take Gordon and me to Gleneagles for a day's golf, playing a round on the King's course in the morning and, after lunch at the Clubhouse, a round on the Queen's in the afternoon. These were the days before golf buggies, either hand-drawn or motorised, and it was customary at Gleneagles

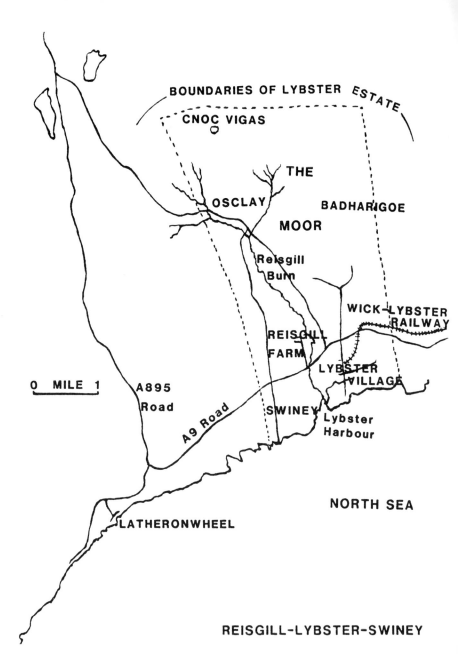

BOUNDARIES OF LYBSTER ESTATE

CNOC VIGAS

THE

OSCLAY

BADHARIGOE

MOOR

Reisgill
Burn

WICK-LYBSTER
RAILWAY

REISGILL
FARM

LYBSTER
VILLAGE

0 MILE 1

A895
Road

A9 Road

SWINEY

Lybster
Harbour

NORTH SEA

LATHERONWHEEL

REISGILL-LYBSTER-SWINEY

MAP 3:   Map of Reisgill, Lybster and Swiney Estate, Caithness.

46

to hire a caddie. On one occasion, after hitting what was for me a reasonable drive I walked up to my ball and tentatively suggested to my caddie that I might try a No. 2 iron in an attempt to reach the green. 'Na! Na! laddie' was the reply as he handed me my No. 5 iron, 'you're ower far tae run it up and if you gie the ba' a proper skelp you'll land the bloody thing in Loch Lomon!'.

Summer holidays, and as I grew older some Christmas holidays, were spent with Dan, my 'real' father, at Reisgill farm in Caithness. This entailed an overnight rail journey leaving Buchanan St. Station, Glasgow, at 9.15 p.m. and arriving at Wick around 2 p.m. next day. 'Around 2 p.m.' because north of Inverness time was less urgent and not such an important consideration as in the south – and guards or engine drivers often had topics of importance to discuss with the stationmasters of the various small stations scattered along the railway line. A restaurant car was attached to the train at Inverness and breakfast was served as we skirted the shores of the Beauly Firth, Cromarty Firth and Dornoch Firth *en route* for Bonar Bridge, Lairg, Golspie, Brora and Helmsdale – almost on the boundary of Caithness. Although Helmsdale is only some thirty-seven miles by road from Wick, the railway takes a wide loop inland through the moors of Sutherlandshire and Caithness, stopping at the small stations of Kildonan, Kinbrace, Forsinard, Altnabreac – what splendid names! On either side of the carriage there is nothing but moor, burns, and lochans with at intervals cuttings lined by pallisades of wood to prevent snow drifting on to the railway line in winter. Leaving the train at Wick, my rail journey was not yet completed because I then transferred to a branch line which went back along the coast thirteen miles to Lybster. This line, the last to be built in the north and opened in 1903, was closed in 1943. At Lybster I would be met by pony and trap, in later years by car, and conveyed the one and a half miles (2.4 kilometres) to Reisgill (*see Map 3*).

Reisgill was the home farm of Reisgill, Lybster and Swiney Estates and had been in my family since 1922. The entire property comprised 1700 acres, the home farm accounting for some 200 acres. Apart from Lybster village, crofts were scattered over the arable coastal strip while inland this yielded to the moor – 'the hill'.

This was no waste-land but formed, rather, an essential part of the estate's economy, providing pasture for the Cheviot and Cheviot-Border Leicester sheep, fuel in the form of peat for Reisgill, and the various crofts as part of their tenantry rights, and grouse because Lybster was a shooting moor. The moor was leased from August 12th each year, the opening of the grouse shooting season, to a shooting party, usually some wealthy Englishman and his friends, who stayed for the Season at the Portland Arms Hotel, Lybster. A grouse moor requires a gamekeeper and kennels in the same way as Cheviot sheep require a shepherd and his sheepdogs. On Lybster both gamekeeper and shepherd lived on the moor at Osclay and Badharigoe respectively and were important and highly respected individuals.

My holidays at Reisgill were a delightful mixture of working on the farm, particularly with horses, riding, fishing, golfing on Lybster's nine hole course, and shooting. In the pre-tractor era, Reisgill and horses were synonymous. My father bred Clydesdale horses and I suppose there were four classes of horses on the farm at any one time. The work force comprised five Clydesdales — *Jock*, a massive brown gelding, *Miss* and *Fancy*, two brown mares, *Jean*, a black mare and *Daisy* a roan. The aristocrats were a handful of well bred ladies who, at intervals, presented my father with a foal, the sires being imported into the county from the south, usually the Borders, for a period each year. These ladies were rather disdainfully presssed into service at times of maximum activity such as harvesting the corn crop and I recall the foals under those circumstances regarding their mothers with anxious eyes and pricked ears from an adjoining field. Of these ladies, *Lady Ardyne* was the most distinguished, having defeated the Duke of Portland's entries at the local Show on three successive years.

The third category were the yearlings, an amiable crowd of loafers, not yet broken in, and living off the fat of the land. One year when I was eleven or twelve years old I became rather attached to some half-a-dozen Clydesdale yearlings who frequented a field immediately above Reisgill House. I paid my respects to them each day and although not broken in, they knew me and after the manner of the breed were quiet and good natured. One evening after supper

I had an irresistable desire to ride one. My particular fancy was a roan gelding and he was sufficiently quiet for me to mount by climbing on to a stone dyke and then transferring to his back, his very broad back. He remained unperturbed and plodded up the field like an elderly cow. At the top of the sloping field he turned, still quiet and amiable to face downhill. Then, as if entering into the spirit of the thing, he started off at a clumping trot which broke into a gallop. We careered downhill, with no bridle or halter, my hands entwined in his mane and my sense of balance working overtime, until at the foot dyke the good fellow slithered to a stop and I stared into the eyes of my father standing on the other side of the dyke. On such occasions greetings such as 'Good evening, Sir' are superflous. I was directed to the estate office. There, in a voice which on occasion had reduced tough game dogs and collies to whimpering wrecks, I was given a lecture which had a similar effect on me. Dan, my father, did not shout but there was an inflexion in his deep resonant, scornful, 'biting voice which had an awesome effect on man and beast.

JMS on Daisy, a 'thoroughly evil' Shetland pony, at Reisgill House,
Caithness.
Left to right: a friend, my grandmother, my uncle Peter (Sutherland),
JMS, and father (Donald Sutherland). Photo, circa 1927.

The fourth category of horses were 'the pensioners' including a hackney mare *Skyline* and her daughter *Sheila*, a cross with a Highland pony sire, and my mount when I outgrew *Daisy*, a thorougly evil Shetland pony on which I learned to ride. My father was of the view that it was safer and better to learn to ride bareback, without saddle or stirrups which in a fall might snare a foot. *Daisy* took full advantage of this so that when she was tired of being ridden, or in a bad humour, she would execute a smart right or left turn and then prop. Since she was as round as a butterball there was no way of staying on board and as I 'ran out of horse' the evil creature would contrive to get in a swift bite on my gluteus maximus.

The great social events of the summer season in Caithness were the agricultural–horse shows held in July–August each year before the busy harvest season. With breeders of Clydesdale horses there was always a considerable rivalry and for some weeks before each show horses would be brought to peak condition, washed and groomed, their great hairy feet shampooed, dried with sawdust, brushed out, powdered with talc and then brushed again so that the hair almost covered the hooves. The hooves themselves would be trimmed and new shoes fitted at the blacksmith's smithy. A visit to the smithy was the occasion of one of my proudest moments. One summer when I was aged eleven or thereabouts, I was asked to take *Lady Ardyne* to the blacksmith to be newly shod prior to a Show. Normally the grieve himself or one of the men would have done this but some farm crisis must have arisen such as a dry spell in which to 'get the hay in before the Show', which necessitated all hands on deck. *Lady Ardyne's* foal was put in a loose box and I was a proud lad as I walked the half mile up the county road to Swiney where 'Billy the Smith's' smithy was situated. These were the days of 'hot shoeing', so that once the old shoes were removed and the wall of the hoof trimmed with nippers and rasp, a strip of metal was put into the forge and heated to 'white heat' with the aid of a huge bellows, until malleable. It was then removed by long tongs and held firmly on the anvil while beaten into shape. The shoe was then plunged into a bucket of cold water and applied while still hot to the animal's hoof, with a sizzle and the acrid smell of burned hoof, but with no pain to the horse. This process would be repeated,

50

heatings, hammerings and fittings, until 'Billy the Smith' was satisfied that he had achieved a perfect fit. Then it was all repeated for the other three hooves.

All went well at the smithy, but on the way back to Reisgill, *Lady Ardyne* became increasingly restive, probably from the combined effects of knowing she was returning to her great gangling 'baby' and from the discomfort of an uncomfortably full udder. At any rate, the good lady crab walked, neighed, puffed, blew and sweated. I felt rather like an ineffectual tug-boat trying to manœuvre a liner. As this was in August, there was a considerable number of visitors' cars on the road and whether they were impressed or horrified at a small lad's attempts to control a huge sweating Clydesdale I will never know. Actually, *Lady Ardyne* was too well trained for there to be any problem; she was simply showing off and indicating her need to return to her family.

For local shows at Lybster, or Latheron, the horses were walked early on the morning of the show to their destination and it was quite a thrill seeing half a dozen magnificent creatures walking in line out of the stable yard. For the county shows at Thurso or Wick, two or three Clydesdale mares with their foals would be loaded on to a railway horsebox carriage at Lybster and taken to the Showgrounds on the day prior to the event. At these shows I usually had a foal to lead and generally care for. One year I had a very handsome young foal in my charge, one of *Lady Ardyne's* best but considered too young to be judged. The final judging of mares with foals at foot was taking place. We were standing in line waiting for the final decision of the judges. The animals had already walked and trotted before the judge, they had been prodded, and poked, their mouths examined, their hooves inspected and generally carefully assessed. It was all too much for my young charge. The poor little fellow simply lay down beside his mother and went to sleep. It was too late to try to get him on his feet — the judges had stopped at us. One of the great men briefly looked down at me and said, smiling, 'Don't worry, son, he'll get up when he's ready. I'm thinking you will be sleeping soundly yourself, this night'. At the end of the day I had no prize ribbons or tickets with which to adorn my little chap's halter. I raided the sheep and cattle pens, returning

51

John Sutherland with 'piny foalie'.

Agricultural Show, Thurso, circa 1933

with a number of 'Firsts' and a 'Supreme Champion' card which I attached to the colt's halter. I was duly rewarded as we walked through the streets of Wick by cries of 'My, look at that piny [small] foalie wi' a' the tickets on 'im!'

It is not my intention to attempt to defend blood sports but rather to describe a way of life in the Highlands before World War II.

Mr Alexander Grant, gamekeeper, came to Lybster from the Duke of Portland's Berriedale properties when my father acquired the estate in 1923, and there he remained, although for a number of years retired, until his death in 1961. He was a stocky, fresh complexioned man, always dressed in heather mixture plus four tweeds and, as befitted his status, invariably wore a collar and tie. A fine shot himself, Alec taught me as a lad how to shoot and care for firearms. My first gun was a 410 double barrel shot gun and I later graduated to the customary 12 bore gun. He was a strict instructor. When walking on the moor the safety catch had to be 'on': when crossing a fence, dyke or deep ditch the gun had to be unloaded; woe betide me if the weapon, loaded or unloaded, was inadvertently pointed at man or dog. I can still hear Alec's soft Highland accent if I failed to unload crossing a fence:

*Well, well, now Mr John, you must be feeling real
bad and you too tired to unload your gun. We will
chust be going home now.*

Alec was responsible for organising burning heather on parts
of the moor each year to ensure a supply of fresh young heather for
grouse to feed on. He discouraged human poachers and animal or
bird predators and each year he was responsible for estimating the
number of grouse which could be shot that season, the number of
brace being the basis for the shooting tenant's rent. Alec was also in
charge of the shooting party and he was an absolute ruler in his own
domain, the moor. His word was law, even to the extent of limiting
the shooting to 'cocks only' or ceasing it entirely if he felt the
remaining birds were necessary for breeding purposes irrespective of
whether or not the anticipated 'bag' had been achieved.

Grouse are shot in three principal ways. On large estates the
'guns' walk or are driven to shooting butts, small enclosures constructed of turf and heather of sufficient size to house one or two
'guns' and their loaders. The grouse are then driven towards these
strategically placed butts by a line of beaters. On small shoots the
usual method is simply to 'walk up' the birds while the third method,
and that employed on Lybster, was to 'shoot over dogs'. It was an
entrancing sight to see a well trained pointer or setter ranging from
side to side some thirty to forty yards out from the line of 'guns' as
the 'guns' walked across the moor under the direction of the gamekeeper. Suddenly, the dog stands motionless like a statue, head and
nose extended, tail straight beind, in front of a heather clad peat
bank. Mr Grant walks slowly up to the dog murmuring a reassuring
'steady, boy, steady'. The animal takes a few steps forward, then a
few more, the shooting party standing in line behind the 'keeper' and
his dog. All at once a covey of grouse explodes from the heather.
The pointer lies motionless as the rather 'flat' reports of 12 bore
shot guns follow and several grouse crumble in the air before falling
to the heather. Then, at the 'keeper's' command, the dog gillie slips
one of the two glossy black labradors held on leash with the other
setters. No commands are necessary; she has already 'marked' where
the birds have fallen and after nosing into the heather she gently

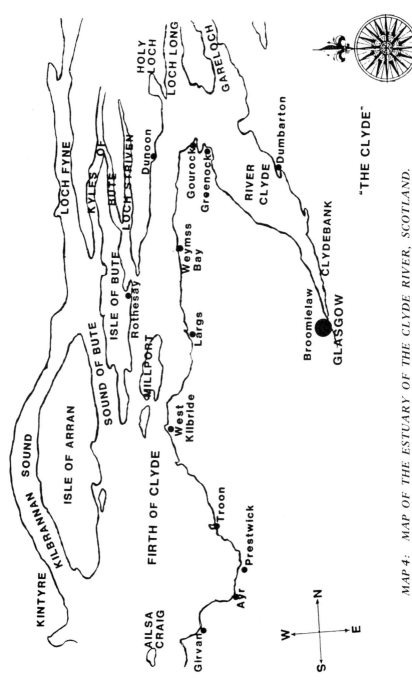

MAP 4: MAP OF THE ESTUARY OF THE CLYDE RIVER, SCOTLAND.

picks up a dead bird and brings it back to the gamekeeper's hand.

My own shooting was only rarely of this kind. Alec Grant and I would go out with perhaps a setter and a spaniel and shoot rabbits, hares, grouse or partridges 'for the pot' or to give to friends. On Lybster, there was no hand rearing of game birds. When shot over, and cared for to the extent of controlling foxes, wildcats, crows and the like and ensuring a good supply of young heather to feed on by burning off old heather, three to five hundred brace of grouse together with partridge, snipe, rabbit and hare could be culled each year. Now trees have replaced the heather. With no gamekeeper, vermin abound. Artificially introduced myxomatosis virtually wiped out the rabbit population. Game has disappeared, and with it part of the Highland way of life.

Part of the Highland way of life, pre World War II days, was also loyalty. Servants perhaps, but servile never, men like Mr Grant, gamekeeper, Mr Spence, grieve [farm overseer], Mr Sutherland, shepherd, were experts in their respective fields and were treated as such. They gave unswerving loyalty to my father and his interests. In return, they were regarded as members of the family.

*

Easter holidays usually saw my Aunt and I (joined by my Uncle at weekends), and often accompanied by friends, spend a couple of weeks at one of the Clyde resorts, generally Rothesay or Dunoon. If fate was kind to me we sailed by paddle steamer from the Broomielaw, Glasgow, all the way to our destination, but if less fortunate, and this was usually the case as my Aunt was a poor sailor, a train journey to a port further down the Clyde estuary, then a shorter sea trip was the start of the holiday, a start tinged with regret at having to forgo the added thrill of a meal on the steamer.

Sailing down the River Clyde on a pleasant spring day in the 1920s and '30s was a colourful and exciting experience. In the days before British Rail, Scotland was well served by two private enterprise Railway Companies – LMS (London Midland and Scottish), and LNER (London and North Eastern Railway), and both companies operated ships on the Clyde estuary, the majority being paddle steamers. The LMS vessels had yellow funnels with black tops and were named after aristocracy or the Gods — for example, *Duchess of Montrose, Jupiter* and *Mercury*, while the LNER steamers had red funnels topped white and black, and were named after Sir Walter Scott's poems and novels, such as *Marmion* and *Waverley*. Two other companies operated passenger ships, Williamson's with black topped white funnels and the majestic *Columba* and *Iona*, which with the *Davaar* and *Dalriada* carried on the Clyde the red, black topped funnels of MacBraynes. These vessels made a colourful sight as, crowded with holidaymakers, they made their way to the many resorts on the Clyde estuary — Kirn, Dunoon, Rothesay or to Brodick and Lamlash on the Isle of Arran, and far away Campbelltown at the foot of Kintyre, or took passengers on a cruise around Bute (*see Map 4*).

After leaving the Broomielaw, the *Queen Mary*, or *Queen Elizabeth* might have been seen building in John Brown's shipyard at Clydebank while further down river, at the *Tail of the Bank* on the port side, cargo ships from all over the world would be busily engaged discharging or taking on cargo at Greenock and Gourock, regarded rather disdainfully by a P and O liner lying off shore waiting to embark her passengers. If lucky, on looking north there might be a battleship or cruiser silhouetted against the sparkling waters of the Holy Loch and Loch Long, framed by the distant Highland hills. In the 1930s the scene was saddened by scores of redundant merchant ships lying, rotting at buoys in all the lochs of the Clyde estuary. They were to be needed ere long.

Having so frequently enjoyed the Clyde, a quirk of fate saw me in August, 1944, lying off Gourock in a troopship waiting while the convoy assembled with no shore leave allowed — and only two weeks after my wedding. Eventually, in the gathering dusk of an August evening, we sailed down the Firth of Clyde with Arran and Ailsa Craig to starboard, Largs, Troon, Prestwick, Ayr, Girvan and all the golf courses I knew so well to port, *en route* to the Mediterranean.

In the 1930s, there lived in the same district of Glasgow as my friends and I, a bevy of young ladies. In 1933, I returned from Caithness to be met with the startling news that my friends had made contact with this clutch of chicks. Apparently, Ian and Gordon, in the absence of my guiding hand and under the strong influence of their wakening endocrine systems, had spoken to the young ladies while walking home in the same direction from a cinema show which both boys and girls had attended quite independently. The girls had chatted back. Contact was established. The ice of adolescence had been broken.

In due course, I was introduced to Pat, Nancy, Jean, Peggy and Bettine. There was no immediate burgeoning of romance between Pat and me but I was much impressed by the salutary effect the young ladies had on some of our football players, when they graced a match with their presence. I recall, for example, how Rowell Lockhart (sadly killed in action in Italy, while serving with the London Scottish Regiment) amazed us all with the upturn of his form — and all because of Jean.

Our social outings with our new friends were limited to occasional visits to a cinema, the annual school ball held in the Assembly Hall at High School, and occasional form dances invariably held at the *Plaza, Palais de Dance*. These dances called for some crafty jockeying for a partner. Ian Thomson, Gordon Stuart, Rowell Lockhart, Charles Dunbar and yours truly vieing for the favours of Pat, Nancy, Peggy, Jean or Bettine. Although partnered off for the occasion, we would go to the function and sit together in a group and always have at least one dance with our friends' partners. Teenagers at this time were unsophisticated. Our romances were on a very platonic level — even at the University in my year of 188 male and 45 female students there were no marriages and only a couple of engagements. There was no alcohol sold at *The Plaza* and drug taking was unknown. We danced, in compatible company, waltzes, foxtrots, tangos, rhumbas and the like to the music made famous by the 'Big Bands', such as Ambrose, Geraldo, Harry Roy, Roy Fox in Britain, and Duke Ellington, Louis Armstrong, Harry James and others in America, and at every dance there was a quota of 'old fashioned' dances (Pride of Erin,

St Bernard's Waltz), and Highland dances (notably the Eightsome Reel).

Walter Templeton, later to survive the War serving in the 9th Commando Regiment, but at the time an erstwhile 'poet', was so moved by the pairing of our group of boys and girls that he was stimulated to write some doggerel about each couple. Possibly because our romance tended to fluctuate wildly, Pat and I were accorded these lines:

> *John and Pat Campbell*
> *Their love is a gamble*
> *Here today; gone tomorrow*
> *It will only bring them infinite sorrow!*

In these pages I have attempted to describe life as I knew it in suburban and rural Scotland during the first thirty-nine years of the 20th Century. One of the greatest differences between the first and second halves of the century must lie in the field of transport.

In the first half of the century, the British Railways network offered a reliable, comfortable and fast means of transport throughout the country with reasonably priced branch line connections to many remote parts. Partly because of this, partly because of neglected roads during World War I, and partly because of expense allied to unreliability, cars were relatively uncommon. The first car owned by my father was an 'Argyll'. This make of car was manufactured in Scotland at Alexandria, near Glasgow, from about 1900, and by 1913 the Company was the fifth largest manufacturer of cars in Britain. Unfortunately, competition became too intense; the Company ceased to exist in 1930, and with it died hopes of a car industry in Scotland.

My father later 'went off' cars, preferring a pony and trap for local journeys, hiring a car when necessary, and travelling to Wick by the branch line railway which had been opened in 1903. Private motoring in Britain was, however, given a tremendous impetus by the general strike of 1926, since many people avoided some of the effects of this industrial action, notably the absence of public transport, by travelling to and from work in motor vehicles. This was the start in Britain of commuter travel by car and was to usher in the 'Golden age of motoring' which lasted until the outbreak of World War II.

Despite the 1930s being the zenith of this 'Golden age', although perhaps because of it — cars were relatively uncommon, only one person in every 30.6 in Britain owning a motor vehicle. In comparison, the average number of people to each car in the United States of America was 5.6, followed by New Zealand with 10.5 per car, while Australia had 13.8 persons to each car. This relative lack of private motor transport was reflected in the fact that, together with my uncle Peter, only two or three other families in my group of friends owned a car while a second car in the family was virtually unknown in middle class Scotland. There was certainly no question of any of us being given, or expecting, a car on turning seventeen years of age but we did have the use of the family car on occasions such as going to golf or taking our partner and another couple to a dance.

Prior to 1930 there was no compulsory insurance against accidents and before 1936 anyone aged seventeen years or over was eligible to hold a driving licence without a test, as I recall, on the annual payment of seven shillings and sixpence. Not until 1936 was a speed limit of 30 m.p.h. imposed in 'built up areas', and elsewhere one could drive as fast as the car was capable of or the road would allow. 'Police traps', however, did exist and traffic laws were so

One of the Sutherland's early cars, a Fiat.

Photographed at Reisgill, Caithness.

out-dated that it was extremely easy to break the law and be charged with 'dangerous driving'. To circumvent this hazard it was prudent to join the Automobile Association (AA), or the Royal Automobile Club (RAC). Both organisations had motorcycle patrols and on passing a member's car sporting the appropriate badge it was customary for the patrolman to salute. If he did not, the implication was that something was amiss — such as a police trap operating in the vicinity.

In 1935–36, the cheapest car available in Britain was the Ford 'Popular' of 8 HP selling at one hundred pounds, closely followed by the Morris '8' at one hundred and thirty-two pounds sterling. Both firms manufactured more up-market models and, indeed, in the 1930s, three hundred to six hundred pounds would purchase a prestige car. There were some 60–70 makes to choose from and there were still more expensive models such as Daimlers, Bentleys, Rolls-Royce and imported exotica such as Bugatti, costing in excess of one thousand pounds, available to the well-heeled motorist of that day.

In the 1930s petrol cost one shilling to one shilling and three-pence per gallon, depending on the brand and the octane rating. It is difficult now to contemplate life in a motoring Elysium where one could purchase a new car for two hundred dollars, fill the petrol tank at 24 cents per gallon, travel through a city with no traffic lights (police directed the flow of traffic at busy intersections), park almost anywhere (no parking meters!), and on leaving the city travel at any speed you deemed appropriate and of which the car was capable without fear of radar traps and with relatively little traffic to inconvenience you. However, the cars of the '30s, were less reliable and slower than today's models. Road holding was relatively poor, tyres less durable and more liable to punctures, while roads were narrower and frequently poorly surfaced. Freeways, motorways, even four-lane highways were in the future. Hills appeared steeper; on ascending them radiators boiled; on descending them drum brakes had a tendency to overheat and 'fade' with marked loss of efficiency.

In the 1930s, there was a challenge, even a feeling of adventure, in undertaking a journey of, say, 300 miles from Glasgow to Caithness. To recapture something of motoring in the 1930s, I would

THE FINAL YEAR FORM AT GLASGOW HIGH SCHOOL, 1937.
JMS, middle row, second right.

*(Included in the photograph are: Hugh Roberts; W. Thorburn; Gordon W. Stuart;
John Rowell; Thomas A. Smith; William Barclay; H.M. Sinclair; M. Stone;
John Wilkinson; James H. Sharpe; James Roy; A. Wotherspoon;
Alex M. Ritchie.)*

commend the fifty-six miles of road from Invermoriston (south of Inverness and on the western bank of Loch Ness), to Kyle of Lochalsh and the ferry to Skye. This road was originally constructed by General Wade and is the original 'Road to the Isles', as well as the road followed by Johnson and Boswell in 1773. Taking your time because the road is narrow and has passing places, you will have opportunity to admire Loch Clunie, Glen Shiel, Loch Duich and the mountains – 'The five sisters of Kintail' which enclose them. Passing through Dornie and Balmacarra, an understanding of the 'Tangle of the Isles' will begin and its magic will grow as the road drops down into Kyle of Lochalsh, with the Isle of Skye and the Cuchullin Mountains on its doorstep. And so on the threshold of Skye which I was to know so well a decade later, I must take a lingering farewell to the '20s and '30s. In July, 1937, I completed my school career and took off for Caithness determined to join the faculty of veterinary science of Glasgow University. During that vacation I was converted to human medicine, I suspect by the combined efforts of my father and his friend (and mine), Dr Walter Ramsay, a general practitioner of Wick. I had frequently stayed for a week or so with the Ramsays during summer vacations. An ex-boxing and football blue of Edinburgh University, an excellent shot, a keen fisherman and a lover

of 'Alvis' cars, Walter was on a pedestal as far as I was concerned and when he said, 'Don't be so bloody silly: you're not going to be a vet, you are going to do Medicine', the die was cast.

Unfortunately, when I applied to the Faculty of Medicine, the year was full and I was advised to enrol in a BSc course. This I did and, despite having little in common with Lord Kelvin and Natural Philosophy, I did sufficiently well to transfer to medicine in 1938.

Dr Walter Ramsay (left), a general practitioner of Wick, and John Sutherland. Photo, at Wick, 1937.

GLASGOW UNIVERSITY AND THE WESTERN INFIRMARY, GLASGOW, 1938-1944

Nineteen thirty eight was a dismal year for us in Britain. In March we witnessed the German invasion of Austria, the dissolution of the Austrian Republic, and the annexation of its territory to the German Reich. In September, following the Munich agreement between Chamberlain and Daladier, Hitler and Mussolini, Czechoslavakia was thrown to German, Polish and Hungarian wolves by Chamberlain and Daladier, in exchange for what Mr Chamberlain believed would be 'peace for our time'. But it was not to be. One year later, at dawn on September 1st, 1939, German forces invaded Poland and on September 3rd, listening to the radio with my 'parents', Peter and Jessie Sutherland, we heard Neville Chamberlain solemnly and sadly announce that a state of war existed between us and Germany. With these words the way of life we had known and enjoyed came abruptly to an end.

By 1940 Britain was fighting for survival. The German Army had overrun the Low Countries and Belgium. France was collapsing. In June, an Army of 335,490 officers and men was successfully evacuated from Dunkirk, although 30,000 men and most of the Army's equipment remained in France. Against this background Mr Winston Churchill, now Prime Minister of Britain, delivered an historic speech to the House of Commons, but addressed to the Nation and to the World, which included these passages:

A Far Off Sunlit Place

> *We are told that Herr Hitler has a plan for invading the British Isles ... Even although large tracts of Europe and many old famous states have fallen ... we shall not flag or fail. We shall go on to the end. We shall fight in France, we shall fight on the seas and oceans, we shall fight with growing confidence and growing strength in the air, we shall defend our Island whatever the cost may be. We shall fight on the beaches, we shall fight on the landing grounds, we shall fight in the fields and on the streets, we shall fight in the hills; we shall never surrender.*

These words convey how close Britain was to being invaded, but from July to September, 1940, the Royal Air Force's 'finest hour' won the Battle of Britain in the skies over the British Isles and the English Channel. This victory, at the cost of 915 RAF planes and 1733 German aircraft, was commensurate in importance with the defeat of the Spanish Armada 352 years before. Hitler's planned invasion of Britain, 'Operation Sea Lion' was postponed indefinitely.

Thereafter, for a year and until Hitler made his fatal mistake of invading Russia, Britain, the Dominions and Colonies faced the might of Germany alone. In the British Isles, Hitler's 'War of total annihilation against the enemies of the German Reich' rained bombs on cities and civilians while, out in the Atlantic Ocean, German U boats attempted to starve the British Isles into submission. As a result food, clothes, soap, coal, petrol, indeed all essential commodities, were rationed or on 'coupons'. Travel was restricted and, since the North of Scotland was a 'Prohibited Zone', I had to obtain a permit to travel to Caithness.

Because of air-raids a strict blackout was enforced. There was no street lighting. Shop windows were unlit and often boarded up. The windows and doors of homes were heavily screened to prevent any light escaping and Air Raid Wardens patrolling the streets ensured that this was obeyed. The headlights of cars and buses were hooded to allow only a slit of light, directed towards the ground, to escape, and eventually there were no private cars on the roads, petrol coupons being issued only for essential purposes. Since the outbreak of war conscription for all healthy males was in force and conscription for females soon followed, the ladies joining the Armed Forces – the WRNS, the ATS, the WAAFS or being directed into munition factories or the Land Army. Public transport was restricted; trains were overcrowded and at night carriages were lit only by one small blue ceiling light, the corridors on long distance trains being packed with troops in complete darkness.

This was the picture in the British Isles from 1940 to 1945, yet despite air raids, food shortages, conscription and hardship, or perhaps because of them, there existed a splendid camaraderie which only rarely surfaces in times of peace.

On a broader front, throughout 1941 and 1942, the Eighth Army, based on Egypt, was locked in a see-saw conflict with German forces under General Rommel in North Africa, culminating in the Battle of El Alamein in October, 1942, followed by the fall of Tunis, and the liberation of North Africa in 1943. In 1941, Russia and the United States were drawn into the War by Germany invading Russia on June 22nd and by the Japanese bombing Pearl Harbour on December 7th and invading Malaysia on December 8th. As Mr Churchill wrote in *The Second World War* volume 3, –

> *Many disasters, immeasurable cost and tribulation lay ahead, but there was no more doubt about the end ... we should emerge, however mauled or mutilated, safe and victorious.*

And mauled we were ... the loss of HMS *Hood* in May, 1941, and HMS *Repulse* and *Prince of Wales* in December, were cruel blows, while the impossible happened when Singapore surrendered to the Japanese in early 1942.

Happier events were to follow. In 1943, Allied armies invaded Italy and at Stalingrad the remnants of the German Army which had invested the city surrendered to the Russians. On July 4th, 1944, as I was having breakfast in the Western Infirmary, Glasgow, the wireless announced that the Allied invasion of Europe was under-way – D Day of the 'Second Front' had arrived.

Having completed a year of pure science in 1937–38, I commenced in 1938 the first year of the five year medical course of Botany, Zoology, Medical Physics and Medical Chemistry. Since I had already passed the first two subjects in pure science, first year medicine was an easy year.

Partly because of this, partly because I had been in the Officers Training Corps at school, but largely because of the excellent Clubhouse facilities on campus, I joined the University Officers Training Corps. For some reason, possibly because of an unerring skill at 'reading' contour maps and placing regimental aid posts in the direct line of enemy fire, I topped the Certificate A examinations and as a reward was invited (that is, ordered) to spend two weeks during the forthcoming University vacation at the Royal Army Medical Corps Depot near Aldershot. I was required to travel in uniform and for the first time in his life Corporal Sutherland was let loose in London dressed in khaki tunic and the kilt, I think, of the Argyll and Sutherland Highlanders. As I had to spend one night in London before reporting to the Depot, I checked in at the Services 'Union Jack Club', opposite Waterloo Station, and then to pass the evening went to a cinema. As I threaded my way along a row of seats in the stalls I was horrified to experience someone making an attempt to discover what Scotsmen wore under their kilt.

At the RAMC Depot the group of OTC medical students from various Universities, of which I was a member, was introduced to regular army physical training. This is what decided me to join the Navy, eventually. Conducted by a Regular Army PT instructor whose only conversation at 7 a.m. each morning was 'Good morning, Gentlemen', for an hour we were never allowed to stand still. Even when being instructed in the next exercise we had to continue 'running on the spot' ("Up! Up! Up!, my young doctors!") or perform 'Legs astride, legs together' ("Come on! Put some effort into it while I am talking!"), and all this followed by a run during which we were abused into alternately jogging and sprinting. One of the group sustained some injury or other in a game of football against a team from the Officers Mess and was admitted to the Cambridge Hospital, Aldershot. Two of us elected to visit him on Saturday afternoon and while walking to town dressed in 'civies' we passed a racecourse. Shortly afterwards there was a thud of hooves from a horse that had broken free and who was now enthusiastically engaged in putting distance between himself and the racecourse. For some reason I have never been able to fathom I grabbed the trailing reins as the animal cantered past and hung on. Fortunately, the creature had the good sense to come to a halt and we stood eyeing each other as a car with the trainer on board drew up. He was most civil and grateful and his hand was drawing his wallet out of his pocket when he asked '... and where are you chaps from?' 'Officers Training Corps, RAMC Depot', we chirruped. 'Oh sorry, doctors! I was about to insult you' said the trainer, returning the wallet to his pocket. Little did he know how welcome some largess would have been to impecunious medical students.

Second year professional courses, comprising five terms of Anatomy and three of Physiology, commenced in January, 1939, the year being interrupted by the outbreak of war in September. As a member of the University OTC, I was required to report to OTC headquarters in the event of hostilities being declared and some days later I was interviewed and provisionally enlisted with a preference for the Royal Tank Corps. Some time after this, however, I received a document to the effect that as a second year medical student I was at present exempt from military service and my call-up would be deferred until six months after I qualified, provided I did not fail a year during the medical course.

Ian Thomson was by this time in Fiji and joined the Pacific Regiment, seeing action in the Solomon Islands against the Japanese. Charles Dunbar, whose parents were both doctors, had unwillingly become a medical student, and he now took the opportunity of failing second year, joined the Army, served with distinction throughout the War and, remaining in the Service, was to become a Major-General, Royal Scots Fusiliers. Gordon Stuart enlised in the Highland Light Infantry, Rowell Lockhart in the London Scottish Regiment (neither survived the War), Gordon Watson in the Argyll and Sutherland Highlanders while Walter Templeton became a Commando. A few of my friends, Gordon Lindsay, Bill Thorburn, David Barclay, all second year medical students, continued at

University feeling, with the hundred odd other males of the year, somehow 'out of it'.

Second year was a grind and I should think that our introduction to the anatomy dissecting room must have left an indelible impression on most. The room was a large laboratory with some twenty bodies preserved in formalin laid out on mortuary tables. We worked in groups, one group dissecting 'head and neck', others 'thorax and abdomen', 'leg', 'arm', rather like busy little maggots eating their way into a body.

In third year one could see the way ahead in that Pathology taught us for the first time in the course about diseases, materia medica and therapeutics about the drugs available to combat them and, as this year merged into the clinical years, we came into contact with actual patients in the wards of the Glasgow teaching hospitals. We carried stethoscopes (rather ostentatiously), listened to hearts, palpated abdomens, witnessed operations and felt at last we were getting somewhere.

During these years Pat, then my girl friend, was initially in Edinburgh, gaining her Princess Louise Nursing Certificate, later working with Dr Adam Barr, an eminent Glasgow obstetrician and gynaecologist. In December, 1942 she joined the Women's Royal Naval Service. Although stationed in Glasgow, she served 'Watch on, Watch off' which did not leave much time for romance to flourish. But flourish it did and we reached an 'understanding' that we would become engaged when I qualified – to become 'engaged', far less married, until qualified and earning money was unheard of.

It was in my third year that I encountered a doctor who was to influence greatly my subsequent career. Francis Esmond Reynolds, an Edinburgh graduate, was senior pathologist to the City of Glasgow Municipal Hospitals, and a Medical Examiner to the Crown. He had just failed to secure the Chair of Pathology in Edinburgh prior to coming to Glasgow and, basically a neuropathologist, had become a highly regarded forensic pathologist. I was delighted when he invited me to work in his department at Stobhill Hospital as an unpaid staff member during vacations. This opportunity furnished me with a good grounding in pathology, sowed the seeds of my later interest in neurology and medico-legal work, and gained me a First

Class Honours in Pathology. I greatly admired F.E. Reynolds; we golfed together, I visited his home, we became good friends despite the disparity in ages; had it not been for the war, I might have become a forensic pathologist.

Glasgow, like Edinburgh which has the Senior Chair of Forensic Medicine in Great Britain, made famous by men such as Harvey Littlejohn and Sydney Smith, had a considerable reputation in Medical Jurisprudence largely due to the two Professors John Glaister, father and son. The son was the incumbent of the Chair when I was an undergraduate and he had a flair, a panache, which made him a formidable witness.

> *But, Professor, I put it to you, you cannot be expected to know much about a greyhound's coat?*
> *Sir, I am an expert on the integument of all mammals from the duck-billed platypus to the primates!*

The father, Professor John Glaister, Senior, who was even more of a character, was immortalised in a poem of at least twenty-three verses, anonymous but attributed to O.H. Mavor (James Bridie, the playwright) and Walter Elliot, parliamentarian, at the time both undergraduates at the University. I can give you only a sample:

> *I'm the Professor of Medical Ju,*
> *A fact which I duly impress upon you,*
> *I never get flurried whatever I do,*
> *For I am the great Professor John Glaister,*
> *Just bear that in mind and you're sure to get through.*
>
> *Now please understand I'm a self made MD,*
> *I'm DPH (Cambridge) and FRSE,*
> *And if I should live to the next Century,*
> *They're certain to make me the first Baron Glaister*
> *A thing which is fitting as fitting could be.*

If you chance to expire in a manner that's queer,
If you're shrivelled by lightning or poisoned by beer,
At the Fiscal's injunction I probe and I peer,
In all of the organs of all cavities
'Till the proximate cause of your demise is clear.

After that the verses become increasingly 'medical' and 'forensic'.

It was Dr Reynolds who introduced me to Dr D.K. Adams, physician with a strong leaning to neurology, at the Western Infirmary, and Stobhill Hospital, Glasgow. Both Reynolds and Adams held each other in high regard and I was strongly advised by Dr Reynolds to attempt to secure a place in Dr Adam's clinic at the Western Infirmary for my clinical medicine course. After the manner of the day, students applied for acceptance in the clinic of their choice and since D.K. Adams was a popular teacher I was fortunate in obtaining a place in his clinic in both fourth and fifth years.

In these pre-National Health Service days the senior doctor of a Unit, 'the Chief', was at the apex of a pyramidal system which comprised the Unit's hierarchy, and virtually could choose his own staff. Undoubtedly, he could make – or break a young doctor. I was therefore very fortunate when 'DK', as Dr Adams was universally known, paid me the signal honour in fifth year of inviting me to be his Resident Medical Officer when – and if – I qualified in October, 1943.

Douglas Kinchin Adams, MA, BSc, MD, FRCP *Lond.*, FRFPSG, was a brilliant clinician with a difficult personality. He tended to be moody, prone to intense likes and dislikes and was blessed with a tremendous command of English while cursed with a withering tongue. From the point of view of a student he was, however, an outstanding teacher and much of what I learned and subsequently taught my students and young colleagues emanated from DK. His favourite dictum was that in all walks of life one must observe, assess evidence and draw reasonable deductions. I hear a voice from the past saying,

> *Remember this, Sutherland, and remember it well;*
> *the ability to assess evidence and to reach a valid*
> *conclusion is a fundamental principle of efficient*
> *medical practice.*

An intense admirer of the 'greats' in medicine, Sir William Macewen, Sir William Osler, 'that great man Gowers', Sir Henry Head, Sir Robert Muir and the like, he had little time for those he termed, however unjustly, 'fashionable doctors'.

> **Student:** *I read that Lord Dawson of Penn said ...*
> **DK:** *Ha! I tell you Mr Brown, Dawson's only original*
> *contribution to the medical literature was his*
> *notice, 'The King's life is drawing peacefully to an*
> *end' as King George V was dying in 1932!*

I did not see much of Rear Admiral Sir John McNee, Regius Professor of Medicine. Regius Chairs are appointed by the Crown, although the University is usually asked to advise the Crown about the appointment. He did give some lectures but was normally occupied with administrative work and with his wartime naval duties. His 'quote' in our Final year Faculty of Medicine 1938–43, souvenir read:

> *They tell me that the Admiral is as nice as he can be,*
> *But we've never seen the Admiral, for the Admiral has*
> *never been to sea.*   — Popular song.

The story goes — and it may be apocryphal, that Professor G.B. Fleming of Child Health, at the outbreak of war and in a bout of patriotic fervour, presented his Rolls Royce to the Government. He was, however, not amused some days later to see Sir John McNee being driven in it by a Royal Navy driver.

The fourth professional courses included Surgery, Midwifery and Gynaecology, Vaccination, Ophthalmology, Venereal Diseases, Tuberculosis, Diseases of the Ear, Nose and Throat, Mental Disease, Fevers, and Diseases of Children, which extended from 1941 through into 1943.

The midwifery course required us to attend a number of cases of labour and to conduct a certain number of labour cases personally. This was termed 'being on district', because the deliveries occurred in the patients' homes in the poorer districts of Glasgow. For this part of the course students were based on the Women's Hospital, Rottenrow, Glasgow, and on being notified of the impending event would cycle to the appropriate address. An alternative was to attend the Rotunda Hospital, Dublin, where a similar course took place and which was accepted by the University of Glasgow, the Rotunda Hospital for long having held a leading place in midwifery in Europe. As Eire was not at war with the Axis Powers, this alternative had the advantage of a temporary return to peace time, no air-raids, no blackouts, no rationing — better food, and Guinness stout! After securing the necessary permit a number of us sailed from Glasgow to Belfast, and thence travelled by train to Dublin. Southern Ireland was a foreign, almost continental country to us but the Irish are a kindly people (despite the activities at the present time of extremists on both sides), and we enjoyed our stay at the Rotunda although, having lived in a total war environment for three years, it was rather hard to take some characters on the streets of Dublin sporting Swastika badges in their buttonholes.

As our fourth year ended and we proceeded into our Final Year the '38—43' year of 108 male and 45 female students became a closely knit group. Somewhere along the way we had adopted as a 'signature tune', a song, 'There's an old mill by the stream, Nellie Dean' which in fourth and fifth years we would sing before each University lecture. The effect on the various lecturers was an interesting study. Some of the 'better' men would join in the singing or, like old Dr Donald MacIntyre, obstetrician and gynaecologist, would make us repeat it if they felt the singing was not up to scratch. Others would look pained, wince and tap a foot impatiently until it ended. Still others would walk out until '... you're my heart's desire, I love you Nellie Dean' rolled around the lecture theatre when they would reappear. We even treated the dignitaries at our Graduation Ceremony to a particularly fine rendition. I think many parents attending the ceremony must have been horrified at seeing and hearing 'their young doctors' behaving in this unprincipled and unprofessional manner.

As I recall, the Final Year finished in July, and in September the final written, clinical and oral examinations in medicine (including child health), surgery and midwifery were held. Before burning the midnight oil, Gordon Lindsay, David Barclay and I spent a week at Leven on the Fifeshire coast where we played golf on the Leven links all day and drank beer each evening. During that week a Fair was being held near the hotel where the three of us shared an attic room and one evening as we drifted (or floated) around the Fair, it appeared appropriate as our Finals were only a few weeks away to have our fortunes told. We made one stipulation to our gypsy fortune teller; the three of us must be allowed to remain in the tent while she told our individual fortunes in case any bad news which she might have to impart would have a detrimental effect on a colleague's health and render immediate restorative treatment necessary. After agreeing unwillingly to do this, she gave us great hope by assuring us of success, fame and fortune ending, however, at the end of each 'fortune', with 'Beware! You have one weakness ... the demon drink'. I recall thinking at the time 'What a clever woman! What a remarkable gift!' But in retrospect how she was able to carry on with her act while three medical students exhaled beer-laden breath in the narrow confines of her tent arouses admiration.

The date when the results of the Finals would be announced was known and it was customary for the names of the successful candidates to be posted on the Faculty Notice Board about 10 a.m., too late for that morning's papers. I can recall clearly that very long tramcar journey from Newlands to the University, and as I walked up University Avenue, a number of my colleagues walking down, called 'You're through, John.' I still had to see the notice with my own eyes to appreciate that 'Sutherland John MacKay' was no longer a mere medical student distrusted by mothers and suspected by fathers but a fully qualified member of an honourable profession. The greatest professional hurdle was a thing of the past, but never to be forgotten.

In retrospect I cannot say I did not enjoy my undergraduate career, but how much better it might have been. The main problem was the onus our very special dispensation placed on us allied to, I suppose, almost a feeling of guilt when one encountered the parents

John MacKay Sutherland
Final Year Dinner, as a medical student
on graduation, October 1943.

of a friend who was on active service. In much lesser degree, the general environment, shortages, the absence of things we had once taken for granted, extracurricular duties such as fire watching at the University, and attending the local Air Raid First Aid Centre when air raid sirens gave warning of a raid, did not make for a particularly happy undergraduate career. We all recognised, however, how fortunate we were at being able to complete our course and hopefully, then, being able to join one of the Services.

I graduated MB, ChB on 23rd October, 1943, and shortly afterwards took up my appointment as Resident Medical Officer to Dr D.K. Adams, Western Infirmary, Glasgow, at the princely salary of one pound per week — but sixpence was deducted for laundry.

On Christmas Day, 1943, Pat and I became officially engaged to be married.

I was elated on the morning I took up my duties in Wards 2 and 7 at the Western Infirmary, and even my chief's admonition 'Remember Sutherland, food and sleep are privileges', did nothing to dampen my enthusiasm. I soon discovered that DK was not exaggerating. Ward 7 was the male ward with a 'normal' complement of some thirty beds. Ward 2 was the female counterpart and my quarters, a bedroom, sitting room and bathroom, were situated between the wards along with a small laboratory, a side room capable of housing two patients and the usual ward offices including Sister's room, kitchen and the like. Although strategically placed in the event of an emergency occurring in either ward, I was vulnerable to being disturbed by the night staff and it was rare to enjoy an undisturbed night's sleep. I became adept at 'cat-napping' and of wakening, fully aware, at any hour, a facility which has continued with me to this day. There was no official 'on duty' or 'off duty'. A Western Infirmary resident doctor (RMO) of the 1943-44 era was on duty all the time and if you had a 'big date' and left the hospital, you arranged for a colleague to be 'on call' for you – and naturally *vice versa.*

Rotating with the other three medical units, we admitted patients every fourth day. The other units were headed by Professor Sir John William McNee, Dr John Gracie and Dr William Snodgrass. Yes! Just like the television series 'Dr Finlay's Case Book', we had a 'Snoddie' and I am not sure if the television specialist was not modelled on our Consultant physician. The Western Infirmary's Dr Snodgrass was an excellent physician but appeared to be a cold, aloof, humourless character and, although superficially polite to each other, there was no love lost between DK and Snoddie. One day DK and I passed Dr Snodgrass and his entourage in a corridor of the hospital,

Patricia Campbell, my future wife.
At the time of our engagement,
December 1943.

the two chiefs according each other the most perfunctory of nods and a brief 'Morning'. We had no sooner passed when in a carrying voice Dr Adams queried 'Tell me Sutherland, was that "Snod" or "God".'

Each day, with the exception of Saturdays and Sundays, Dr Adams paid a ward visit, arriving punctually at 9 a.m. and departing at 11.30 a.m., and for this he was paid añ honorarium of something like one hundred pounds per annum. Yet, despite this lack of financial reward there was an intense rivalry to obtain, and immense kudos in being, a consulting physician or surgeon to a teaching hospital. Without this achievement, you were not really practising in the 'First Division'.

Everything had to be on top line for 'the Chief's visit'. A typical ward visit might go something like this — DK being accompanied by Sister, six senior medical students and myself:

DK (to the first patient):	*Morning.*
and to me,	*What is the problem?*
JMS:	*Well Sir ......*
DK:	*Angels and Minister of Grace defend us! When you start a sentence with 'Well' Sutherland, I know ill is bound to follow!*
JMS:	*You remember. Sir ...*
DK:	*No! I don't remember!*
JMS	*Sir, this is a patient with symptoms suggestive of a duodenal ulcer. You requested a barium meal. The result confirms the diagnosis.*
DK:	*As I thought,* [and turning to the students] *Mr Jones you have heard what Dr Sutherland has said. Now, from your intensive study of the literature on duodenal ulceration, perhaps you would enlighten us with an account of the medical treatment of this condition.*

And so from bed to bed; sometimes lighter moments occurred:

DK: *Who reported this case? Mr Brown. Is Mr
Brown here? Ah! Here he comes. Ultimus
Romanorum! Brown who lives but a stone's
throw from the Infirmary, the son of a doctor
who has been on his rounds hours ago, slinks
in half-an-hour late!*

At this stage a student rattles the fender surrounding the fireplace
which with its chimney occupies the centre of the ward:

DK: *There goes that Devil's tattoo again! Come
out of the fire, you salamander! Come near
the patient, a knowledge of clinical medicine
will never ooze into you from afar.
You will recall this patient who was admitted
with attacks of stabbing pains in his legs, an
unsteady gait, unsteadiness of balance
induced by eye closure — the so called
Romberg test although the good Lord knows
that the significance of unsteadiness when
closing the eyes while washing the face in the
in the morning over the washbasin was
recognised long before Romberg. This patient
also had absent knee and ankle jerks and
vibration and joint position sensibilities were
impaired in his legs. Mr Smith, we achieved a
diagnosis of tabes dorsalis without the help of
Dr Wassermann, although his test added
further evidence in support of our opinion;
now would you be good enough to inform us
of the four essential changes in the pupils
described by Dr Argyll-Robertson in such
cases?*

At the end of the visit, having seen each patient in both wards, Dr
Adams would retire to the chief's room; his staff would join him;
Sister would serve tea and then punctually at 11.30 a.m. I would

accompany him, carrying his case, to his car. This would now seem servile but none of us resented this custom of 'seeing the chief off' – or of carrying his case.

My six months with Dr Adams sped by. In contrast with student life which was accompanied by a sense of guilt at not being, like so many of our friends, in the Services we felt that as RMOs we were already doing something worthwhile and that in a few weeks or months we would also be in uniform. At 'The Western' each RMO knew his colleagues intimately. It was traditional at that time that no lady doctor was appointed to the resident staff of the Western Infirmary (and indeed I know of no female on the visiting medical staff) so we house physicians and surgeons, some twenty strong, were indeed a band of brothers proud to be staff members, however lowly, of a famous hospital. We enjoyed 'living in' a hospital mess life which has now largely departed from the medical scene.

The nursing staff of the Western Infirmary were carefully selected and proved to be happy and efficient girls, while the Sisters were experienced and helpful to their young doctors. The nursing staff 'lived in' at the Nurses Home – strictly 'off limits' to the doctors, but on the wards and no matter how busy they were there was always a cup of tea to hand if they had to rouse you from your slumbers to see a patient or if you came in late from a rare evening out.

During my six months as an RMO, I applied for and was accepted for service in the Royal Navy. Always a bit superior even in war time, the Navy required a reference as to one's fitness to be a member of the Senior Service. Dr Adams dictated this, my first medical reference, which I have retained with some pride:

> *I have pleasure in stating that Dr John Sutherland has been personally known to me for some years past, both as a junior and also as a senior student.*
>
> *I thought so highly of his abilities that I offered him the appointment of House Physician in my wards at the Western Infirmary, as from November, 1943, and he is still acting in that capacity. During this period Dr Sutherland has performed his work to my entire*

satisfaction. I have a very high opinion of his ability, industry and character. I have found him entirely conscientious and efficient and he has always proved a most loyal and courteous colleague. He is exceptionally well qualified for a Commission and I wish him every success.

[Signed] *Douglas Adams, MA, BSc, MD ChB, FRCP (Lond).*

31 March, 1944

Almost twenty-eight years previously Douglas Adams had himself been at sea and 31 May, 1916 saw him in one of Admiral Beatty's battle cruisers heading at full speed to join forces with the Grand Fleet under the command of Admiral Jellicoe off the Skaggerak and Jutland — ('What an awe inspiring sight it was to see the masts of the Grand Fleet on the horizon'). He therefore had empathy for someone about to join the same Service, following in his footsteps. For my own part I felt really important when DK would announce to some visitor or other 'Sutherland is just about to join the Fleet'.

And so ended my first appointment to Dr Adam's staff. I admired him greatly and owe a debt of gratitude to him as a teacher, my chief, and, in due course, my friend.

The wedding of John MacKay Sutherland and Patricia Campbell.
Dr and Mrs John Sutherland with their Guard-of-Honour at The Congregational Church,
Polloksbields, Glasgow, 27 July 1944.

A FAR OFF SUNLIT PLACE

SURGEON LIEUTENANT RNVR

TO

Surgeon Lieutenant John MacKay Sutherland MB ChB, RNVR
The Lords Commissioners of the Admiralty hereby appoint
you Probationary Temporary Surgeon Lieutenant RNVR of
His Majesty's Ship 'Drake' for RN Barracks Devonport and direct
you to repair to your duties on 9th June, 1944.

BY COMMAND OF THEIR LORDSHIPS.

When I joined the Royal Navy in June, 1944, the war in Europe had less than a year to run. The war against Germany ended officially one minute past midnight on May 8, 1945, and four months later on September 2, VJ Day was celebrated. The Normandy invasion following D Day had gone well. The Russians had forced the Germans back into Germany. The Allied advance up Italy continued, while on the other side of the Adriatic the war in Yugoslavia was gaining in dimension and Greece had been liberated. In the far East, the British Army recaptured Burma from the Japanese and the United States won several key naval battles. The Battle of the Coral Sea in May, 1942 forced the Japanese to abandon their amphibious expedition against Port Moresby. The losses they then sustained may well have been a critical factor in the decisive American victory of

81

Midway one month later, in which Japan lost four aircraft carriers and the cream of her aircraft carrier pilots. The biggest naval battle in history, in terms of the forces involved and the area over which it ranged, occurred in October, 1944 in the Gulf of Leyte in the Philippines. In this action, after which the Japanese Navy ceased to play a significant role in the war, American naval ships and aircraft sank three battleships, four aircraft carriers, ten cruisers and nine destroyers, losing in the process one light carrier and two escort carriers, two destroyers and one destroyer-escort. On August 6th and 9th, 1945, American aircraft dropped atomic bombs on Japan and on August 14th Japan unconditionally surrendered.

Looking back on the dark days of 1940 when Winston Churchill made his famous 'We shall never surrender' speech we, that is Britain, the Commonwealth, the Colonies and in due course the Allies, had achieved a famous victory, but not without cost. The Battle in the Atlantic and other oceans against German and Italian U boats lasted from the first day of the war to peace being declared. In the course of this unremitting struggle 2,828 merchant ships were lost. The cost to the Royal Navy in the war amounted to 5 battleships, 7 aircraft carriers, 28 cruisers, 128 destroyers, 67 submarines, 14 armed merchant cruisers, 29 corvettes, 2 sloops, 30 fleet sweepers and 175 trawlers. It could truly be said 'If blood be the price of Admiralty, Lord God we ha' paid in full' (Rudyard Kipling).

At the Royal Naval Barracks, Devonport, near Plymouth, the recent intake of medical officers, of which I was one, were fitted out by Gieves and given a few weeks indoctrination into the traditions of the Service and its customs, a course in gas warfare, and lectures relevant to the health of a Ship's Company. As a gesture to our own survival, a chief Petty Officer ensured that we could swim the length of the swimming pool fully clothed. From time to time we medically checked the crew of a ship commissioning or de-commissioning and while so engaged on one occasion I saw an elderly Surgeon Commander RN 'listening' to a sailor's heart and lungs with the earpieces of his stethoscope firmly plugged into the sides of his neck!

In due course I was handed the following, dated July 21, 1944:

By Command of the Commissioners for Executing the Office of Lord High Admiral of the United Kingdom etc.
To

Surgeon Lieutenant J. MacK. Sutherland MB ChB, RNVR
The Lords Commissioners of the Admiralty hereby appoint you
To His Majesty's Ship 'Lauderdale' and direct you to repair on board that Ship on the Mediterranean Station.
Your appointment is to take effect from 25 July, 1944, and vice Whiston and you will be required to be in readiness to leave at an early date.

On receipt of my orders I was granted leave, experiencing emotions no doubt similar to those felt by Horatio, Admiral Lord Nelson, when he was appointed to his first ship in a manner and style very similar to mine.

My embarkation leave was subject to immediate recall and I was not permitted to travel beyond a radius of fifty miles from Glasgow. Despite this Pat and I planned an immediate wedding which duly took place at the Congregational Church, Pollokshields, Glasgow, on July 27th, 1944.

Arranging for a honeymoon within the prescribed fifty miles limit proved more difficult because July and August are holiday months in Scotland and, what with travel restrictions and lack of petrol, all accommodation within easy reach of Glasgow was fully booked. In some desperation we telephoned a hotel in Biggar, a pleasant country town at the foothills of the Borders almost equidistant between Edinburgh and Glasgow. Although listed in the Automobile Association Annual book of 1939 as an hotel, the Station Hotel, Biggar, had unknown to us been requisitioned and occupied by a Girls' Boarding School, evacuated from Edinburgh because of the risk of air raids. In July the School was on vacation

SURGEON LIEUTENANT JOHN SUTHERLAND RNVR, 1944

and the only residents of the School buildings were two teachers, a mother and daughter. Dear Souls! They took pity on us and at one stroke we became the only 'hotel' guests they ever had and the only couple I know of who honeymooned at a Girls' School.

Although Biggar is, perhaps, an unlikely place for a honeymoon we enjoyed every precious minute of it, minutes made more precious by our delight on returning to our 'hotel' from a walk to discover that no recall telegram awaited us. I say 'us' because Pat was a member of the Womens' Royal Naval Service (WRNS) and had been given compassionate leave for her wedding, subject to recall – some of her friends termed it 'passionate leave'! In the event we had our week's honeymoon but eventually *the* telegram arrived and by an irony of fate I boarded a troopship (the ex P & O *Strathmore*) at Gourock where a convoy for the Middle East was assembling, on August 20th, 1944, my 25th birthday, and by chance Pat was recalled to night duty at her WRNS Signal Station on the same day. The irony did not cease. From working in Signals Pat was well aware that the convoy continued to assemble in the estuary of the Clyde for some five days after I boarded the *Strathmore*. Pat could not

Leading Wren Patricia Sutherland

get aboard. No shore leave was allowed. I was so near yet so far from my bonny bride.

One evening with the sun setting behind the Arran hills the convoy sailed down the Firth of Clyde and then, to minimise the risk of U boat attack, northwards round the North of Ireland and so into the Atlantic. In due course we slipped through the Straits of Gibraltar, again at dusk, into the Mediterranean and then along the North African coast to Port Said where we disembarked, a voyage of over four weeks from joining the *Strathmore* at Gourock (*see Map 5*).

The trip was uneventful, n'er a U boat or enemy aircraft seen or heard – at least by the passengers. At Gourock my rank of Surgeon Lieutenant had been misread as Sub Lieutenant and I was assigned sleeping quarters on the *Strathmore* which I shared with

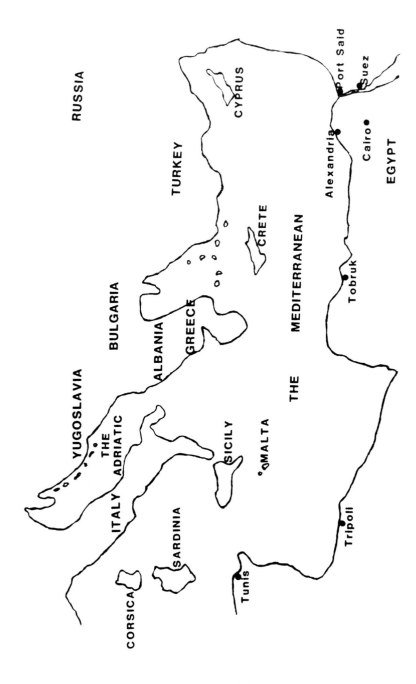

MAP 5: *Map of the Mediterranean, showing operational theatres of war, 1944.*

four or five naval Warrant and Chief Petty Officers. The mistake was discovered and I was offered a cabin shared with another lieutenant. This I declined, thereby making one of the better decisions of my naval career. The Warrant and Chief Petty Officers had all been in the Service 'man and boy', and over the ensuing weeks they put me wise to many customs, wrinkles and dodges that I might otherwise never have learned. I was a 'new chum' in their profession and they were older, wiser and senior to me in all matters pertaining to the Navy except rank and they took me, as it were, under their wing. I enjoyed their company as I enjoyed playing bridge each evening with a Surgeon Lieutenant Commander RN and two RNVR types, one a barrister in London. No money passed hands in our bridge games but scores were kept and at Port Said after four weeks of playing bridge each evening there was hardly any difference in our individual scores.

Disembarking at Port Said was one thing, locating HMS *Lauderdale* was quite another. A consensus of opinion at the Naval

HMS Lauderdale entering Grand Harbour, Malta.

Office was that she was bound to turn up at Alexandria where she had boiler cleaned in July, 1944, and so up coast to 'Alex' I travelled in a hot, crowded, dusty train. At Alexandria no one knew of *Lauderdale's* whereabouts. One school of thought held that she had been sunk with all hands while another was of the view she was engaged in some private enterprise such as 'running' condoms to Yugoslavia!

Such is naval humour and feeling somewhat outré and unwanted I fetched up in rather pleasant quarters at Ras el Tin lighthouse, then a naval station, until some days later a signal arrived despatching me to Cairo 'to await further orders'. After a pleasant enough stay in Cairo at a hostelry with the somewhat unlikely name of *The Essex House Hotel* I (and my prickly heat) found ourselves consigned to Bari, Italy, via an RAF 'Dakota' of Transport Command. There I exchanged the discomforts of the 'Dakota', with its canvas seating along the sides of the fuselage and an 'Elsan' type dry toilet secured to the deck at the rear of the 'plane, for the terrors of being driven from Bari to Taranto in an army lorry driven by an Italian who considered himself a spiritual descendant of Nuvolari. And so it was in the evening of 15th September, 1944, I first saw *Lauderdale* lying stern to quay in Taranto Harbour. The colours were being lowered. A boatswain's pipe was sounding and various characters were standing to attention or saluting ... altogether, I remember thinking, a rather first class welcome! (*See Maps 5 and 6*)

HMS *Lauderdale* was one of a hundred or so Hunt Class destroyers built during the war and named after various Hunts in the British Isles, the Lauderdale Hunt being located in south Scotland near Berwick-on-Tweed. *Lauderdale* was launched at the Southampton yard of Thornycrofts in 1941. As ships-of-war go she was small. Even compared with some other classes of destroyers she was on the diminutive side, being only 280 feet in length, with a beam of 31 feet and a displacement of just over 1000 tons. Equipped with two steam turbine engines developing 19,000 horse power, *Lauderdale's* effective full speed was something in excess of 30 knots — although a request for revolutions for such speed would normally bring 'Chiefy' (the Chief Engineer Officer), hastening to the bridge. For her size she fairly bristled with offensive weapons —

six four inch guns in three twin turrets, a quadruple pom-pom amidships, a single pom-pom for'ard, twin oerlikons on either side of the bridge and 60 depth charges. She did not carry torpedoes.

To deal with all this and with radar, asdic and other equipment some 210 souls including 10 officers constituted the Ship's Complement. In a ship of only 280 feet in length there was not much room to spare. Some 90% of the ship's company were enlisted men – 'Hostilities only' ratings, the remaining 10% being 'Regulars' – chief petty officers, petty officers, chief ERAs and stokers who had been in the services all their adult lives and were, indeed, the backbone of every ship's company.

While a unit of the Royal Navy *Lauderdale* had three captains, all RN; George Pound, who commissioned *Lauderdale*, Roland (Rolly) Boddy who was captain when I joined the ship, and John Benians, under whom I also served and who 'paid off' the ship at Portsmouth in 1945, before re-commissioning her to go to Durban, South Africa, for a major refit before joining the Eastern Fleet.

Destroyers were worked hard during the war years. On January 4, 1942, *Lauderdale* sailed for the Clyde for 'working up' exercises; by April 26, 1944, she had sailed 100,000 miles, equivalent to four and a half times round the globe, and was the first 'Hunt' to cross the Atlantic. In 1946, *Lauderdale* was transferred to the Greek Navy. The pendant number L95 on her sides

Captain George Pound CBE, DSC, RN (Retd), First Captain of HMS Lauderdale and President of the Lauderdale Club.

and stern was erased and bearing a new name *Aegean*, and under a different ensign, she steamed out of Grand Harbour, Malta, on July 9, 1946 for the last time. In 1959, she was returned to the Royal Navy and broken up.

*Officers of
HMS Lauderdale.*

*Shore leave in
Italy, 1944.*

JMS, second left.

HMS *Lauderdale* joined the Mediterranean Fleet in April, 1943, under the command of Captain George Pound. In October of that year his father, Admiral Sir Dudley Pound RN, became terminally ill suffering from a brain tumour; George Pound returned to Britain and Lieutenant R.L. Boddy RN, took over command of *Lauderdale*.

It was to Captain Boddy that I presented myself on the morning of 16th September 1944. Meeting one's first Royal Navy Captain for the first time strikes awe even into a stout Scottish heart. However, on the previous evening I had been made welcome in the wardroom and over several Cyprus brandies had been advised by Lieutenant John Lewis RN (First Lieutenant) and Lieutenant James Jungius RN, how to act and what to say (but not how to say it). Next morning, impeccably turned out by my Sick Bay Attendant, SBA Harry Wright, in civil life a gentleman's gentleman, I knocked at the door of the Captain's cabin and entered. 'Surgeon Lieutenant Sutherland reporting, Sir'. Captain R.L. Boddy (visibly shaken): 'Good God, Doc! I hope you have brought an interpreter with you'.

R.L. Boddy and I became good friends. A doctor, and perhaps particularly an RNVR from 'civvy street' has on a small ship, a rather privileged position and to some extent the Captain can unburden himself and socialise with the doctor rather than with his executive officers. The 'loneliness of command' is a very real thing and perhaps from time to time I did something to relieve Rolly's loneliness. Certainly on 30th November, 1944, St Andrew's Day, while boiler cleaning in Malta, this was accomplished. What with the crew of *Lauderdale* putting down a mutiny on another ship, first evening 'in' after a spell in the Adriatic, and it being St Andrew's Day and all, I felt it incumbent on me when we went ashore to introduce my Captain to the Scottish drink of 'a half and a half pint' (a nip of whisky and a half pint of beer). He took to it like a duck to water.

Only in his late twenties when in command of *Lauderdale*, Boddy was of short stature, slim, very fit, immaculately dressed. He had a tremendous sense of humour and a love of dogs — not a bad combination of virtues. He was the dashing type of destroyer captain of one's imagination and he was, indeed, an expert ship handler. On more than one occasion he brought *Lauderdale* alongside, safely in harbour, when her consorts deemed it more prudent to ride out the storm at sea. His aim was to come alongside in only three movements. If this was accomplished, the story goes, Chiefy stood the Captain a drink; if more than three move-ments were required the gin was on the Skipper.

On March 1, Captain Boddy was relieved by John Benians and in the late '50s left the Service to take up hill farming and forestry in Lochailort, Inverness-shire. He also became involved in 'Outward Bound' and from time to time acted as skipper in luxury yachts cruising the Mediterranean, Adriatic or Caribbean, accom-panied by his wife, Johanne-Marie, who ran the galley — lucky ship!

Captain Benians was a more reserved, somewhat aloof, com-manding officer. He was highly professional and efficient and had come to *Lauderdale* from a larger destroyer, HMS *Wolfhound* and had commanded some seven other

Officers of HMS Lauderdale at Ancona, Italy, in the winter of 1945.

HM ships over the previous eleven years. He was thus an officer of considerable seniority and it says a great deal for John Benians and perhaps also for *Lauderdale* that he has continued to participate in the activities of the 'Lauderdale Club'. John was Captain of *Lauderdale* on VE Day at Ancona and on VJ Day at Casablanca.

Lieutenant Commander Bill Forster RNR was the Engineer Officer. I cannot recall anyone calling him 'Bill'; he was, and still is 'Chiefy' to all of us. Born in 1902, in the north country, he served during the first World War in the Royal Flying Corps and had the rare distinction of wearing the Wings of the RFC above the gold braid of his naval rank. After World War I he trained and served as an engineer officer with the Blue Funnel Line, whose ships plied mainly with the Far East. As Chiefy was wont to say:

Life was one long honeymoon in those days – nine or ten months in the East then home for six to eight weeks.

He became a consultant engineer after leaving the Blue Funnel Line and joined *Lauderdale* in 1943. Older than the rest of us, he was a father figure both to the wardroom and to his own part-of-ship. Chiefy was a big man physically, with a large booming voice and ready laugh and smoked a pipe which was hardly ever out. We were lucky to have Chiefy Forster on board. He is now in retirement at Hamble, near Southampton, sailing his yacht until recently, and determined to drive his Saab until he is eighty-eight.

The other lieutenants were John Lewis (First Lieutenant 'No 1'), Jimmy Jungius (Navigator), and Ian Gardiner, always named 'Blenner' (Gunnery Officer). John Lewis and James George Jungius were RN officers who had been in the Navy since the age of twelve or thirteen years, when as cadets they joined the Royal Naval College, Dartmouth. When I served with them John would have been about twenty-three years of age and Jim celebrated his 21st birthday on *Lauderdale*. Both were professionals and highly capable as well as being good companions and staunch friends. John Lewis retired from the Service with the rank of Commander and became a successful farmer in the south of England, aided by his charming wife, Rosanne. Jim remained in the Service and in the course of time rose to the rank

Lieutenant J. ('Jimmy')
G. Jungius RN.

Navigator of
HMS Lauderdale, 1943.

Vice Admiral
Sir James Jungius,
in retirement in
Cornwall.

and status of Vice Admiral Sir James Jungius RN. He and Lady
Jungius, dear 'Bullet', now live in retirement in his home county,
Cornwall.

Following periods of stress, if I had much to do Jim used to give anaesthetics for me as Harry Wright my SBA had to assist with instruments and the like. My practice was to induce anaesthesia with intravenous 'Pentothal', and Jim would then maintain that happy state by sprinkling ether on a mask placed over the patient's nose and mouth. If there was a bit of a chop and the ship was pitching the anaesthetist tended to inhale a considerable volume of the highly volatile ether and it was often a matter of debate as to whether the patient or Jim was the more deeply anaesthetised. In true Naval fashion Lieutenant Jungius RN always stuck to his post! I have seen him as white as a sheet, his face beaded with perspiration, continuing with grim determination to drip ether on to the patient's mask. In later life it did my reputation no harm when I was able to introduce into a story '... and my anaesthetist, Sir James, at the other end of the table ... '.

The Captain, No 1, and Chiefy each had a cabin and J.G. Jungius slept in his Chart House below the bridge. Ian Gardiner and I

Lt Ian Gardiner RNVR, on the forrard deck of HMS Lauderdale, 1944.

shared the 'Senior Double cabin', while the three sub-lieutenants and midshipman bunked down in a rather larger cabin on the wardroom flat. Ian and I lived pretty well cheek by jowl for some nine months. He was a good shipmate and cabin-mate and we have remained close friends over the years.

The seaman's 24 hour day is divided into watches, five watches of four hours and the evening watch, from 1600 to 2000 hours divided into two watches each of two hours known as the first and last dog watches. I became junior officer of the middle watch, starting at midnight, with Lieutenant Ian Gardiner RNVR as the senior watchkeeping officer. In civil life

Ian was a chartered accountant in the Civil Service and I utilised his professional services regularly when attempting, as Wine Caterer, to balance the wine account. In return, I taught him the rudiments of boxing and we had two pairs of boxing gloves hanging continuously on our cabin door. If he was recalcitrant about doing my accountancy a pair of gloves would be slung in his direction and I would commence to beat the Hell out of him. On the other hand, if he felt I was not showing him the respect he considered due to a Senior Lieutenant, a pair of gloves would be thrown at me and a few crushing blows delivered as I was pulling them on. As our 'ring' was a space of approximately six square feet enclosed by a bunk on each side, a desk along the bulkhead and a second bulkhead housing our washhand basin, there was not much room for fancy footwork in our bouts.

Ian returned to the Civil Service after the War. He is now retired, living in Kent with his wife Ann for nine months of the year and in Spain for the three winter months.

After taking part in the allied landings in Southern France, *Lauderdale* was ordered to Taranto for an overdue refit, returning to sea on 14 October, 1944. From then until May, 1945, the ship was involved in what Captain Boddy has described as a mini war in the Adriatic.

Maps 5 and 6 indicate the theatre of operations. The battle lines were the Eighth Army advancing slowly up the east coast of Italy and, across the Adriatic, Yugoslav resistance under Tito, which with the help of British coastal forces, Commando and Long Range Desert Group units was hardening into offensive action. In opposition were the German forces on the mainland of Yugoslavia and in the Dalmatian Islands. They were a resolute and resourceful enemy and in no way a spent force. As pressure on them increased, however, and they started to retreat they became more ruthless and we began to learn of atrocities committed on defenceless islanders prior to their withdrawal.

The German lines of communication and supply were essentially coastal convoys which utilised the inner channel between the islands and the mainland. These convoys were protected by E boats, mobile 88 mm guns on the coastal road, a number of

MAP 6: *The Adriatic Sea, theatre of operations of HMS Lauderdale and her crew, October 1944–May 1945.*
"The War in the Adriatic"

ex-Italian corvettes and destroyers and mine fields. In order to secure the passages through to the inner channel the Germans had established on the islands a number of strong points and gun batteries.

Based on the island of Vis were British motor gun boats (MGBs), motor torpedo boats (MTBs), a number of landing craft equipped with two 4.7 inch guns and rocket firing landing craft, under the command of Lieutenant Commander Morgan Giles. The destroyers, the Hunt class *Lauderdale, Eggesford, Blackmore, Aldenham, Wheatland* and *Avondale,* were in the main based on Brindisi, Bari, and later Ancona under the command of Captain Dickenson, Senior Naval Officer, North Adriatic, while Admiral Morgan (Flag Officer Taranto and Italy – FOTALI) was the overall naval operational commander. The activities of *Lauderdale* and her consorts were numerous – routine patrols to interrupt German lines of communication and support our MGBs, gun fire support for Combined Operations engaged in driving German forces out of the Dalmatian Islands, and bombardment of enemy gun positions defending their convoy routes, sometimes with the assistance of rocket firing landing craft and rocket firing 'Typhoon' planes from, as I recall, a New Zealand squadron. In short, a mixture of routine, cloak and dagger stuff, and bombardments in the confined and heavily mined waters of the Adriatic.

At intervals we would return to Malta to boiler clean or to repair damage. On completion, after three or four days, *Lauderdale* would again sail from Valletta, music from our Hunting Medley record blaring from the ship's loud hailer system across the waters of Grand Harbour and echoing from the walls of a city so steeped in history and so recently besieged by air for three and a half years. In the outer harbour lay the oil tanker *Ohio*. This ship, on loan from America, manned by a British crew and with a British master, in August, 1942 was successfully towed into Grand Harbour by a mine-sweeper and kept afloat largely by destroyers lashed on either side after one of the most bitter convoy battles of the War. The 10,000 tons of fuel she carried was an important factor in enabling Malta to hold out against the incessant Luftwaffe and Italian air force bombing.

My own duties on *Lauderdale* were numerous rather than onerous. I assisted 'Sick Berth Attendant' Harry Wright who was the real 'Doc' in the eyes of the Ship's Company. My other occupations included censoring the mail and being sports officer, wine caterer and junior officer of the middle watch.

Whenever *Lauderdale* anchored off one of the islands I tried to run a surgery either on shore or on board ship to help the local inhabitants, who had not seen a doctor for some years. If the latter, a queue would form outside the surgery while row boats containing more patients circled *Lauderdale* until they were allowed to board. Captain Boddy 'suggested' that I should prepare a report on conditions in the islands and how they might best be remedied with available resources. I did this, using one of the islands as a typical example, and embodied the report in my Journal, a copy of which had to be submitted to the Fleet Medical Officer every three months to acquaint him with what I had been up to during that time. In due course this communication reached me.

From: *Fleet Medical Officer*
              Mediterranean Station
Date: *5th February, 1945*
To: *Surgeon Lieutenant John M Sutherland RNVR*
              HMS Lauderdale

The receipt of the copy of your most interesting and comprehensive Journal for the quarter ending 31st December, 1944 is acknowledged.

The enthusiasm with which you have organised your department of the Ship and the training of certain members of the Ship's company so that they are able to help you in emergencies is most commendable.

The full use you have made of opportunities to study conditions ashore and render assistance to the local inhabitants is noted with approval and your reports on Mulat Island have been read with great interest. It will be passed to the authorities who deal with civilian supplies for their information.

(Signed) *Surgeon Lieutenant Commander RNVR*
           for "Fleet Medical Officer".

I was glad to learn subsequently that the report had been acted upon.

In some instances the 'assistance I gave the local inhabitants' was of a dental nature. Many of the children had never seen a dentist, certainly not for the past three or four years. As a result of this, and of their poor nutrition, caries was rife and many a young Yugoslav suffered the agonies of toothache. Fortunately, the Lords Commissioners of the Admiralty had in their wisdom seen fit to supply *Lauderdale* with a pair of 'forceps dental, universal' and along the Dalmation coast I acquired quite a reputation for being able to separate teeth from their rightful owners. But 'pride goeth before a fall'. On one occasion an aged citizen approached me and indicated with a finger a mouldy looking molar which was apparently causing him trouble. With a cheery 'Not to worry chum' I got to work. I wrenched, pushed, heaved, sweated and swore, but all to no avail. An hour later the wretched molar still leered at me as if pleased at having defied all my efforts to dislodge it. I knew I was beaten, and stepping back, gasped 'I think you had better see your own dentist'. A not inconsiderable feat as the nearest dentist must have been miles away on the mainland behind enemy lines.

However, life on *Lauderdale* had its lighter moments. In November, 1944, in company with *Eggesford* we gave a rather premature Christmas party, each ship entertaining 150 Yugoslav children. Despite the language barrier, a rather severe looking school mistress who acted as interpreter, and a distrustful local political commissar, both the children and the ship's company had a wonderful afternoon. The children were shown a world very different from the one they had so recently lived in. Only a week before they had witnessed parents and other relatives lined up against a wall and shot.

Suddenly it was all over! In April, 1945, Field Marshal Alexander, the Supreme Allied Commander, Mediterranean theatre, issued a Special Order of the Day ... 'Final victory is near. The German Army is very groggy ... ' and on May 3, 1945, the *Union Jack* (the Forces' newspaper) carried the banner headline '**Unconditional Surrender in Italy**' and the information that 'at 12 noon yesterday the capitulation came into effect'.

SPECIAL ORDER OF THE DAY

Soldiers of the Allied Armies in Italy

Final victory is near. The German Army is now very groggy and only needs one mighty punch to knock it out for good. The moment has now come for us to take the field for the last battle which will end the war in Europe. You know what our comrades in the West and in the East are doing on the battlefields. It is now our turn to play our decisive part. It will not be a walk-over; a mortally wounded beast can still be very dangerous. You must be prepared for a hard and bitter fight; but the end is quite certain — there is not the slightest shadow of doubt about that. You, of the famous Allied Armies in Italy who have won every battle you have fought, are going to win this last one.

Forward then into battle with confidence, faith and determination to see it through to the end. Godspeed and good luck to you all.

H.R. Alexander

Field-Marshal,
Supreme Allied Commander,
Mediterranean Theatre.

During these past few months we had lost HMS *Aldenham*, sunk after striking a mine with the loss of seven officers and over one hundred ratings while the Germans lost two destroyers, two corvettes, most of their E boats and numerous land based gun emplacements.

After a channel had been swept clear of mines we were ordered to Trieste, arriving in mid-May, to a very tense situation. The Yugoslavs had occupied the southern and eastern districts of Trieste and were claiming the whole city, the takeover being prevented by General Freyberg's New Zealanders and the Scots Guards. So critical was the situation that *Lauderdale* was allocated a bombardment liaison officer and an armoured car in case open hostilities should break out. This transport was put to very good use in taking bathing parties to a very fine Lido and in conveying *Lauderdale's* medical officer, accompanied by the senior wardroom steward, a Maltese who spoke fluent Italian, into the hinterland in search of vino. The situation continued to be explosive for some time and it was clear that Marshal Tito's partisan forces did not welcome British and Commonwealth troops in Trieste or British warships in the harbour. On one occasion a game of cricket was arranged with an Australian unit. *Lauderdale* won the toss and elected to bat, albeit to my untutored eye none too successfully, when from the security of my armoured car (I had taken a proprietary interest in the vehicle) I saw a platoon of partisans with automatic weapons, hand grenades dangling from their belts – the lot! – filing into Trieste Sports Stadium. They came not as spectators, and with weapons levelled and safety catches off the eleven Australians and the two batsmen were ushered from the oval. In my armoured car I kept a very low profile until the Australian swear words ceased.

The tensions gradually eased and in early June we received a signal to proceed to Port Said to boiler clean before heading for Durban to refit for service with the Eastern Fleet. Before leaving Trieste a Ship's Dance was organised. This was held in a school hall and as the young lady in charge, Claudia Apostoli spoke only Italian and Scots my services were much in demand. On the night of the dance the young ladies brought their mothers along with them – and returned to them after each dance, much to the disappointment of one and all. However, came the interval and supper and, as graphically described by Captain Benians,

> ... *the signorinas, mamas forgotten or trampled under-*
> *foot, fell on the bully beef sandwiches like a pack of*
> *ravening wolves. The Germans certainly kept the civilian*
> *citizens of Trieste hungry during their occupation of*
> *that City.*

Never a very religious ship and, indeed, I recall a Padre being shot by a Very's light (by mistake) when leaving the ship on one occasion, church services were held, however, each Sunday if circumstances permitted. Taken by the Captain, they were brief and to the point but none the less impressive.

The Captain would open with a prayer:

> *O God be good to me*
> *Thy sea is so wide and my ship is so small.*

A hymn would follow, then the reading of the Lesson and another hymn. I still recall snatches of the hymns:

> *O God our help in ages past*
> *Our hope in years to come*

and,

> *Listen while we pray to Thee*
> *For those in peril on the sea.*

Finally, the Naval prayer would be read:

> *O eternal Lord God who alone spreadest out the*
> *heavens and stills the raging of the sea. who has*
> *compassed the waters with bounds until day and night*
> *come to an end. Be pleased to receive into Thy Almighty*
> *and gracious protection the persons of us Thy servants*

and the Fleet in which we serve. that we might be a safeguard to our gracious sovereign Lord, King George and his Dominions and a security for such as pass on the seas on their lawful occasions ... .

Early June, on passage down the Adriatic making for Port Said, a cheer swept through *Lauderdale*. A signal had just been received ordering the ship to proceed to Malta and then home to pay off before recommissioning for service with the Eastern Fleet. When an HM Ship is commissioned a narrow pendant, white with a red cross, flies day and night from the masthead as long as the ship remains in commission. In addition, on a paying off voyage it is customary to fly another pendant made out of sickbay bandages and measuring one yard for every month the ship has been in commission. This pendant is therefore very long and streaming behind the ship it is necessary to give the tail end some buoyancy with an oxygen filled balloon. Condoms filled with sickbay oxygen prove very suitable, although it is impossible to disguise the shape and nature of such balloons. Thus it came about as *Lauderdale* with a 'Whoop! Whoop! Whoop!' of her siren was manoeuvering slowly astern to leave Gibraltar our balloon suspended pendant draped itself across a liberty boat filled with Wrens crossing the harbour. It was to the accompaniment of maidenly shrieks that we set course for Portsmouth.

On July 2, 1945, almost a year after the *Strathmore* had sailed from Gourock, *Lauderdale* lay off Portsmouth Harbour at a buoy and it was there that Pat, still a serving member of the WRNS, managed to get a signal passed to the ship that my avuncular 'father' was critically ill. I was granted immediate leave and was in Glasgow with him for a few days before he died.

After I returned to *Lauderdale* a signal was received on August 2:

Proby temp Surgeon Lt R, Finney RNVR is appointed 'Lauderdale' 7-8-45 and vice Sutherland temp Surgeon Lt. J. McK Sutherland is appointed RN Barracks Portsmouth 9-8-45.

Annually, or on leaving the ship, the commanding officer sends to the Admiralty a confidential report on his officers and the officer is given a 'flimsy' of the CO's general impressions. My two 'flimsys' from *Lauderdale* read:

> ... *has conducted himself to my entire satisfaction. He has taken the greatest care of both the health and welfare of the Ship and has the complete confidence of the Ship's company.*

(**Signed**) R. Boddy, Captain,
4 March, 1945.   HMS Lauderdale.

★

> ... *has conducted himself with great keenness and to my complete satisfaction. A good officer in all respects.*

(**Signed**) J. Benians, Captain,
August 1945.   HMS Lauderdale.

SURGEON LIEUTENANT RNVR :
THE FLEET AIR ARM,
1945-1946

y last appointment in the Royal Navy was to HMS *Siskin*, the RN Air Station, Gosport, and ran from August 13, 1945 to October 26, 1946.

Gosport, Alverstoke and Lee-on-Solent are pleasant districts on the south coast of England, bounded by a long narrow bay which separates them from Portsmouth to the east, by the Solent and Isle of Wight to the south and by Southampton to the west. The airfield at Gosport had a long history. The site was chosen in 1912 as one of the earliest bases of the Royal Flying Corps and it had the distinction of owning a couple of forts, Fort Grange and Fort Rowner, which were built in the 1850s, in the time of Palmerston, as part of the defences of Portsmouth. The cannons with which the forts were originally equipped were never fired in anger but the forts were still in use as storehouses when I was stationed at HMS *Siskin*. A moat surrounded each fort and its still waters proved an ideal breeding ground for mosquitoes. The insecticidal properties of DDT had been discovered about 1940, and by the end of the second World War it was being employed by health authorities in the control of malaria and typhus. I managed to obtain a quantity and I became probably the first naval officer to introduce aerial spraying to combat mosquitoes. This was done by sitting in a helicopter with the door open and, while the pilot slowly circled the moat, a stream

Aerial spraying from the open cockpit — pioneering efforts in mosquito control using DDT. Helicopter aloft at RN Air Station Gosport, in 1946.

of DDT solution was sprayed on to the water and surrounds of the moat by means of a stirrup pump normally used for fire fighting purposes.

The medical staff at RN Air Station, Gosport, comprised a Senior Medical Officer (a Lieutenant Commander RNVR), a medical officer (myself), a dental officer (invariably known in the service as 'toothie'), and a sickbay staff of nine naval sickberth attendants (SBAs) including a Chief Petty Officer, three RAF sick quarters personnel (an RAF Unit was stationed at Gosport) and four ambulance drivers (civilians). The Sick Quarters cum Hospital was spacious and well equipped with an officers' ward of four cots and a ratings ward of twelve, an operating theatre and a dental surgery together with examination rooms, dispensary and offices. With the RN Hospital at Haslar only a few miles away, all this was a far cry from *Lauderdale* with its minute sickbay containing one cot, one operating table, a desk and SBA Harry Wright (and, of course, Sir James), with no one to turn to except *Pye's Surgical Handicraft, Gray's Anatomy* and a well thumbed copy of *Conybeare's Medicine.*

Shortly after September 2, 1945, VJ Day, the SMO was demobbed and returned to general practice in his Welsh hills and I was left as Senior (and only) medical officer of this impressive department – only some two years after qualifying.

HMS *Siskin* was a training rather than an operational station and housed quite a variety of aircraft. A 'Tiger Moth' squadron provided basic flying training for all sub-lieutenants of the regular navy; a 'Fleet requirements squadron' of 'Seafires' (the naval 'Spitfire'); 'Martinets' used for towing targets for gunnery practice; 'Oxfords' for conversion training to multi-engined 'planes and for instrument flying training; a flight of the famous 'Mosquitoes', De Havilland's 440 mph fighter, bomber, photo-reconnaisance 'plane and 'Pathfinder' for the heavy bombers; a flight of Sikorsky helicopters which were used for air-sea rescue – (and DDT spraying!); various other 'planes employed for communication and advanced training. And last, but by no means least, a Fairey 'Swordfish' representative of the 'planes which torpedoed three Italian battleships in Taranto in 1940, the *Bismarck* in 1941, and which when based on Malta were responsible for sinking thousands of tons of enemy shipping. Other activities at *Siskin* included an aircraft torpedo development unit in which the RAF shared, an experimental glider unit, a school of aircraft handling and fire fighting to train deck crews for aircraft carrier duties, and a motorcycling school.

To handle all this, the ship's company mustered well over 1,000. With this number the command structure was very different from that on *Lauderdale*. Flying was supervised by Commander (Air), engine and aircraft maintenance by Commander (Air Engineer) and each squadron or unit had a senior officer, the whole under the command of Captain R. Mills assisted by his Commander, First Lieutenant (a Lieutenant Commander) and their staffs. Captain Mills,

THE MEDICAL STAFF OF RN AIR STATION GOSPORT, IN 1946.
JMS, centre, front row.

the Commander and First Lieutenant, as well as the majority of senior officers, were RN career officers. Ronald Mills was a Captain by rank as well as being Captain of *Siskin*. He was an ex-submariner with a distinguished war record and was every inch of his six feet, a highly competent senior naval officer, strict, just and supportive. As an example of the last, in order to help me cope with the seniority of other department heads, squadron commanders and the like at meetings, he applied to the Admiralty to have me promoted to Surgeon Lieutenant Commander while I occupied my present post. This was turned down, however, on the grounds that no Surgeon Lieutenant under the age of thirty could be promoted beyond that rank. I, therefore, soldiered (?sailored) on as a Temporary Surgeon Lieutenant RNVR (the 'probationary' having already been dropped) until I was demobbed. However, I was given a very pleasant cabin to myself in the Senior Officers Wing at the Wardroom – and my bath was drawn for me each morning. Indeed, I never experienced senior officers in other departments attempting to 'pull rank'; my department was always treated with customary respect and I was invariably addressed as 'Doc' or more formally 'SMO'. What is more, I was allocated a 'Norton' motorbike for my personal use.

After some three-and-a-half years service Pat was demobbed from the WRNS and joined me in the south of England. We secured rooms at Lee-on-Solent in a pleasant little house appropriately named *Arcadia* in Studland Road, owned by a Mrs Carter. Unfortunately, even Arcadians can experience difficulties. One was Mrs Carter's unfortunate habit of turning down the gas under whatever Pat was cooking in the shared kitchen premises; the other was Mrs Carter's large and obnoxious cat called *Dinky*. He and I never really hit it off, perhaps due to my tendency to induce *Dinky* in time honoured fashion to leave our rooms. Fortunately, Mrs Carter never did fathom why *Dinky* arched his back and hissed on encountering me in the hallway.

I 'lived out' unless there was night flying, when I had to be at the Air Station. An ambulance called for me each morning and returned me to Studland Road in the evening. After our evening meal we would often saunter down to the *Inn by the Sea*, a most pleasant hostelry where an evening could be pleasantly spent over a pint of beer chatting to friends from *Siskin* or from the Fleet Air Arm Station, Lee-on-Solent.

Unfortunately this pleasant life was interrupted by Pat having a miscarriage and being admitted to Gosport Hospital for treatment, a civilian hospital, under a very sound gynaecologist. For a time she was really ill and also developed a sensitivity reaction to the sulphonamide preparations she was receiving. Penicillin was at that time still restricted to the armed forces but I had no difficulty in obtaining a supply from the RN Hospital, Haslar and thereafter Pat recovered rapidly. The matron of Gosport Hospital at that time was an autocratic creature who had the local doctors cowed since if any of them displeased her she would refuse to admit his patients. Maybe the National Health Service did some good after all! Pat and I did not see eye to eye with her in many things. One of these was an idiosyncrasy that no recovered patient was allowed to walk out of her hospital; they had to leave the ward on a stretcher or in a wheelchair. This was too much! When Pat was due to be discharged I had one of my 'desert type' ambulances and a stretcher party of four marines attend on the patient. Well primed on the previous evening with libations of beer, the marines marched down the ward in perfect step, wheeled at Pat's bed and at the command 'Stretcher party halt!' did so with the correct stamping of feet. Pat was gently transferred to the stretcher. 'Stretcher party, raise stretcher!' came the command, followed by, 'Stretcher party, quick march! Right wheel!' and so Pat exited from the ward to the applause of patients, past Matron who was on the point of apoplexy, out to the ambulance and back to Lee-on-Solent. As soon as she was in the ambulance, Pat sat up, swung her legs over the side of the stretcher and passed her cigarettes around the marines.

Shortly after this we rented a most attractive home *The Holt* at Alverstoke which was considerably nearer *Siskin*. Because *The Holt* had a garden we decided to purchase a dog which would be company for Pat when I was at the Air Station all day.

We had in mind a terrier perhaps of the Cairn variety and went to kennels advertising 'terriers for sale' in the local paper. The kennel owner took us to a run and on opening the door of the kennel a flood of terriers tumbled out, jumping and sprawling over some obstruction in the doorway as they did so. When the *mêlée* abated, an eight weeks old golden cocker spaniel, looking rather woebegone as only spaniels can, regained his feet and staggered out on puppy legs to greet us. No other dog was looked at. We became the proud owners of a spaniel, rickets and worms being included in the purchase price. The rickets and worms were treated most effectively at the expense of the Royal Navy, via RN Air Station, HMS *Siskin* sick quarters. However, retribution awaited me for misuse of His Majesty's calcium, vitamin D and the popular 'worm medicines' of the day Santonin, elixir of male fern and croton oil.

As befitting the SMO and his wife now that they had a house, we invited the Captain, Commander, the Senior Engineer, Commander, (Air), other notables and their wives for pre-lunch drinks one Sunday morning. While we were preparing savouries and the like for this big social event in our lives, the spaniel puppy (*Tony*) unfortunately had an epileptic fit. I gave him an injection of phenobarbitone and left him to sleep it off just as our guests started to arrive. All was going well; glasses were plenished and replenished, cheerful conversation filled our lounge and in due course questions were asked about our new puppy. 'Can we see the little chap, doc?' asked the Captain. 'Er, sorry Sir. he has been a bit off colour. I've just given him a sedative and he is sound asleep' I replied. Just at that moment the door of the lounge burst open and an excited spaniel puppy barged in, anxious to greet everyone and make them feel at home but, most of all, anxious to get at the grub. A cake stand holding sandwiches and savouries went over, glasses toppled and their contents sloshed on to the floor, while 'the poor, ill, little spaniel' started in on the scattered goodies. I cannot recall having another party at *The Holt*.

Tony however, proved to be a tremendous success and this was particularly the case when our daughter's presence became apparent. Because of the previous miscarriage the obstetrician insisted that Pat rested as much as possible and one can picture the scene each afternoon – the pair of them sharing a bed; *Tony* arranging his flews to his satisfaction and after a last look at his beloved mistress going to sleep with his head on a pillow.

While we were living at Alverstoke my 'mother by arrangement', my Aunt, died and we inherited *Morven.* Because of this, and because we were of a mind that it would be a good thing to have our first child born in Scotland, as August approached Pat and *Tony* returned to Glasgow. Very decently, Pat's brother Bill, a minister in Lerwick, and his wife came down from the Shetland Isles to be with Pat and to look after *Tony* when Pat went into the nursing home.

I had to remain at Gosport but with the blessing of Captain Mills, Commander (Air), arranged for a 'Mosquito' aircraft to take me to Renfrew Airport, Glasgow, as soon as the baby arrived. Arrive Gillian did, on August 12th, 1946 but on that day Gosport and district was enshrouded in fog, all 'planes were grounded and I travelled north by train. I saw Pat and my new daughter briefly before catching the train south again – approximately a 12 hour trip each way instead of just over an hour by 'Mosquito'. My leave had to be brief as orders prohibited flying off or landing on the airfield unless a medical officer was on duty and since I was the sole medical officer at *Siskin* I had to be there – and leave had to be arranged well in advance to secure the services of a relief medical officer.

It was not pleasant being separated from Pat again, and now Gillian, and with the war over I looked forward increasingly to being demobbed and forging a career in civilian life. I enjoyed my life at *Siskin* which was really a form of general practice, as I did being on *Lauderdale*, and I did toy with the idea of a naval career specialising, perhaps, in aviation medicine. However, for a number of years, at least, I would have had to accept sea-going commissions with further separation from wife and family and this persuaded me against such a decision. With hindsight I think thoughts of a naval career held considerable attraction because, whereas I held already some status in the Service, a return to civilian life meant starting once again at the bottom and in an imminent National Health Service, which actually came into being in 1948.

In due course my 'Order for Release from Naval Service' arrived and I left HMS *Siskin* on leave on 28th October, 1946, although not actually demobilised until 23rd December, and then, 'You will be regarded as being in Reserve, and you will be liable to recall to the Naval Service by the revocation of this order at any time', a situation which caused Pat and me some concern in 1956, when we boarded *Oronsay* for Australia at the time of the first Suez crisis.

At a time when officers were being demobilised and leaving *Siskin* almost daily I felt honoured when this note appeared on the Wardroom noticeboard:

Vin D'Honneur
The mess will be at Home at 1215 on Monday 26 October, 1946, to say goodbye to Surgeon Lieutenant JM Sutherland RNVR.

JS Hopkins
Hon. Mess Secretary.

My subsequent rail journey to Scotland passed in a 'blissful state'. I received the usual flimsy on leaving:

Surgeon Lieutenant J.McK Sutherland RNVR has served as Senior Medical Officer in RN Air Station, Gosport, under my command, from 13th day of August, 1945, to 25th day of October, 1946, during which he has conducted himself to my complete satisfaction. A most capable and conscientious medical officer who has filled a position of responsibility with great success and admirable judgement.

(Signed) R. Mills, Captain
25 October 1946 HMS Siskin.

I also appreciated receiving at a later date a personal letter from Captain Mills:

... we were all very sorry to let you go – none sorrier than I was – for we all know you to be a most capable and sympathetic medico besides being our oldest remaining inhabitant.

There is no need for me to wish you luck as a civilian doctor for I know you are fully capable of looking after yourself but I would like to thank you for your loyal service in a one-man practice that may have caused you an occasional moment of anxiety ... I was glad to have an experienced MO to help me.

Give our love to your wife and I hope the young hopeful looks less and less like Pope.

I hope we will meet again.

[Pope was the Commander and rather gnome like – Gillian, my daughter, looked rather like him for a time.]

My naval career ended as it had begun with a message from the Admiralty:

Sir,

I am commanded by my Lords Commissioners of the Admiralty to convey to you an expression of their recognition of your Services in the Royal Navy during the War.

The good wishes of their Lordships go with you on your return to civil life.

I am, Sir
Your obedient servant

11th November, 1946   (**Signed**) *Clifford Marquison.*

June, 1944 to December, 1946, years crowded with events and experiences – our marriage, *Lauderdale*, Malta, Taranto, Bari, Ancona, Trieste, the Dalmation Coast and Islands, the responsibilities of *Siskin*,, the pilots of the Fleet Air Arm, our first home at Alverstoke, Gillian's birth, the deaths of my 'adopted parents' Peter and Jessie Sutherland.

One day after typing *The War Years* Pat said to me –

> *You know, some of the stuff I've been typing will give our young people a funny idea of war. They will think 'fancy having Christmas parties for kids, dances, using an armoured car to collect vino from the farms, playing cricket and so on, when the Navy should have been fighting the enemy and sinking ships.'*

This very reasonable comment gave me pause to think ... my excuse is that the story is being written almost half a century on and with the passage of years kind Nature blunts the recall of less pleasant memories and brings back into focus happy events.

Forgotten are the times on *Lauderdale* when you were so bored that you had a bet with yourself on which cockroach crawling along the bulkhead would reach the deckhead first. Forgotten is the night before some action planned for the following day when the prayer in my heart was echoed in the letters I was censoring,

> *Pray God, keep me safe so that I will get home in one piece.*

I recall, rather, *Lauderdale* with 'The post horn gallop' blaring from her loud hailers sailing proudly out of Grand Harbour. I remember the magic of standing watch with the shadowy figures of the look-outs dimly visible on either wing of the bridge as the darkened ship sliced through the equally dark sea and, as the watch ended, just a suspicion of dawning in the easterly sky. I do not recall except with a sinking feeling hearing on our R/T intercept the German Commander of an E boat informing his colleagues in other boats that he could see two destroyers. I do not want to experience again the revulsion of being shown where Yugoslav men, women and children were shot only a week previously in cold blood. I remember clearly a fellow Scot, a leading-hand in *Lauderdale* but a professional footballer with a leading Scottish Club before the war and a star player in many of the games he played for *Lauderdale*. I do not want to recall his bloated obscene appearance when his body was recovered from the sea about a week after he had been shot in an air-raid and had fallen overboard. I recall happily my little sickbay, Harry Wright SBA assisting, and Lieutenant James Jungius RN giving an anaesthetic, but almost gone are the memories of wounds and burns and the feeling of near desperation I experienced when examining them.

It takes a Robert Graves to paint war as it really is. I am no Graves, but I know war is not something to be enjoyed but endured and endured if necessary by giving kids a party, employing an armoured vehicle to collect vino and so on. To be endured with the help of friendship, comradeship and a pride of belonging. Nature is kind; one recalls how war was endured rather than how it was.

A FAR OFF SUNLIT PLACE

POST WAR SCOTLAND – A DECADE OF MEDICINE 1946-1956

ife is a series of 'ups' and 'downs'. The first 'down' is the almost amoeboid existence of first year at primary school, repeated in the first year of secondary education, as a 'fresher' at University, and as a newly qualified resident in a teaching hospital, albeit in lessening degree. On the other hand, compensation comes with the tremendous seniority of one's last year in primary school, fifth or sixth year of senior school, and as a final year medical student.

I encountered another 'down' on leaving the Navy and the position of SMO of a Fleet Air Arm Station to join a glut of other ex-service doctors looking for jobs and advancement in their profession. The National Health Service was looming large on the horizon and with it, for a number of years, insufficient posts to absorb the number of doctors who had been released from service with the Navy, Army and Air Force. Competition for jobs and appointments was intense. On one occasion, and it was by no means an isolated one, over fifty doctors, some with higher qualifications, applied for a general practice post under the NHS on one of the islands in the Outer Hebrides, a vacancy which it normally would have been difficult to fill.

'Demobbed' doctors were given a three months rehabilitation course, such as being a clinical assistant at a teaching hospital, the rate of remuneration being three hundred and fifty pounds per annum. During this time one was meant to secure some position as an assistant in general practice or, if a future in one of the specialities was envisaged, as a junior registrar in a hospital. In Glasgow an adviser, Professor Noah Morris was available to help plan one's future. I made an appointment to see the professor and told him of my ambition to specialise in medicine and, in particular, in neurology. On learning, however, that I liked the sea and could ride a horse the good professor strongly advised me to apply for a position which was coming up in the Colonial Medical Service, a medical officer in the Falkland Islands ... Fortunately, as my 'rehabilitation' was coming to an end I secured the position of junior registrar (six hundred pounds per annum), and subsequently registrar (seven hundred pounds per annum) in Dr D.K. Adam's Unit and I thus embarked on my second spell of duty at the Western Infirmary, Glasgow.

The position of junior registrar, if I remember correctly, was tenable for one year, that of registrar for two, and senior registrar for three years. During one's senior registrar years in theory one applied for and achieved a consultant post under the NHS somewhere in the United Kingdom. In practice, however, in the 'popular' specialities like medicine and surgery there was a tremendous bottleneck at the senior registrar level. This bottle-neck had at least two results. A higher qualification such as membership of a Royal College of Medicine or a Fellowship of a Royal College of Surgeons was insufficient to secure a consultant post. It was also necessary to have a higher University degree such as MD or to have published a number of worthwhile papers — something to set an applicant apart from his fellows. The second result was that whereas before and during the War there had been much kindness in one's relations with colleagues and considerable humour in everyday life, in the later 1940s 'Every man for himself' epitomised the outlook of many. This led Dr Adams to recall on one occasion that 'Every man for himself' is, in the Royal Navy, the last order of desperation preceding almost certain destruction, a fate which he devoutly hoped would overtake the National Health Service.

During the years 1946–50 I worked at the Western Infirmary

with Dr D.K. Adams and Dr J.B. Gaylor. Dr Adams decreed that while learning my trade in general medicine and neurology with a view to sitting the examination for Membership of the Royal College of Physicians I should undertake research in the hope of submitting a thesis for the degree of MD. In the 1920s Adams had undertaken research work into the aetiology of multiple sclerosis (referred to in Britain at that time as disseminated sclerosis) and had retained a lifelong interest in the disease which he bequeathed to me. For the three years after being appointed to Dr Adam's Unit I carried out investigations into the pathogenesis, clinical factors, serology and treatment of multiple sclerosis.

Statistical analysis of a series of 389 cases of multiple sclerosis led to the conclusion that in Scotland multiple sclerosis had a district incidence; in some areas the disease was common, in others seldom encountered. It also led to an hypothesis that 'infection' was influenced by rural or agricultural exposure and that animals, particularly sheep, might be the natural reservoir of the agent responsible for the disease.

Three diseases of sheep were investigated, louping ill, scrapie and swayback. In collaboration with Dr D.R. Wilson of the Moredun Institute, Edinburgh, an attempt was made in November, 1948, to produce a known pathology in sheep by inoculating six lambs with blood and cerebrospinal fluid from three cases of multiple sclerosis. This was an exciting time because we had reason to feel that we were on the right track in view of a report of the occurrence of multiple sclerosis in four veterinary research officers who had worked on swayback. In the event, analysis of cerebrospinal fluid withdrawn by cisternal puncture from each lamb on two occasions during a 17 month follow-up period was normal and although one lamb developed a meningo-encephalitis the histological appearances of the central nervous system were non-specific and not those of scrapie or swayback – or of multiple sclerosis.

The practical work involved in these investigations was performed during the day when other duties permitted, the reading and writing at home in the evenings. Gillian was only 18–36 months of age during this period and if Pat had an evening out with her girl friends she commonly returned to find her baby propped up in an armchair while I expounded to her the mysteries of multiple sclerosis. Pat and Gillian came to see me receive my Doctorate (with high commendation) in 1950. Both merited an honorary degree for the help they had given me because, in addition to Gillian's interest, Pat had typed the entire draft of the manuscript.

My other 'Chief' was Dr J.B. Gaylor, MA, BSc, MB, ChB, FRCP (Ed), FRCP (Glasg), consultant neurologist to the Western Infirmary and, indeed, the only doctor in the west of Scotland until the end of World War II whose hospital and private practice was restricted solely to neurology.

Although the early decades of the 20th Century have been described as the 'Golden Age of Neurology', paradoxically there were very few neurologists, in the modern sense of the word, in the British Isles or in Australia. Diagnostic neurology, outwith London and its specialised hospitals such as the National Hospital for Nervous Diseases, and the major metropolitan teaching hospitals whose neurologists were also on the staff of one or other of the specialised hospitals, was the province of the general physician with a special interest in, or a flair for, neurology, or of trained neurologists who also practised as general physicians.

J.B. Gaylor was an exception. After qualifying from Glasgow University in 1928, he held house appointments at the Western Infirmary. He then trained in Munich under Spielmeyer, in Utrecht with Boeke, at the National Hospital for Nervous Diseases, London, and at the University of Pennsylvania, before returning to Glasgow in 1938. He was then appointed lecturer in neurology in the Professorial Unit at the Western Infirmary, and in 1941, Neurologist to the Western and Royal Infirmaries and to the Regional Neurosurgical Unit at Killearn Hospital. His private practice was restricted to neurology. An erudite man, an excellent clinician, an expert in electroencephalography and a good companion, I was fortunate to have JB as a mentor, chief and friend. He and D.K. Adams admired and respected each other so that working for both presented no difficulties.

In 1948 I had my first paper published in the *British Medical Journal* of May 1st. It was entitled 'Two cases of polyarteritis nodosa with observations on aetiology, diagnosis and treatment'. Periarteritis or polyarteritis nodosa is an uncommon condition, but by chance two patients who were found to be suffering from this disease were admitted to Dr Adam's Unit within a week or two of each other. I have diagnosed probably only a handful of patients with polyarteritis nodosa in the rest of my career. At any rate, I prepared a paper and proudly presented it to Dr Adams for his approval. A few days later he returned the paper to me at morning tea.

> *Sutherland, I note the word 'draft' on the top left hand corner of the first page : under the circumstances it is as well.*

The years had not mellowed my 'chief'. However, having been reduced in size by about one third, and having wept over the slaughter of my more mellifluent passages, the paper was accepted by the Editor of the *BMJ*. This and similar experiences taught me the value of short words and simple sentences:

Dr Adams pointing to a sentence,

> *What on earth does this gobbledygock mean?*

My reply rather stiffly,

> *It means Sir, we still do not know the cause of multiple sclerosis.*

Dr Adams,

> *Well, merciful heavens, say just that! To think I have tried to teach you for years that words, both spoken and written, are intended to express thought and understanding.*

I would not like to convey the impression that life in these post-war years was unremitting dull drudgery. It was certainly a life of hard work and apart from Saturday nights when we played bridge with friends, or went to the pictures, or had a meal in a restaurant, I worked in my study most evenings.

My colleagues at the Western Infirmary were a good crowd – Ronnie Lendrum, Andrew Muir, Bill Lancaster, Harry Richmond, and a considerable amount of good humoured baiting and gamesmanship went on. The 'chief' had once commented 'a sense of humour is a good index of spiritual integrity – evil men never laugh', and on this basis, in Wards 2 and 7, a high level of spiritual integrity certainly existed.

While I was working on cerebrospinal fluid of sheep a pipette containing cerebrospinal fluid from a sheep with louping ill 'backfired', and fluid entered my mouth. About a week later I developed a typical viral meningitis, a known manifestation of infection with the louping ill virus in humans. Douglas Adams came to *Morven* to see me, considered that I would probably recover and when this eventuated packed me off to Kenmore on Loch Tay for five days convalescence in Highland air. When I returned to work my colleagues greeted me with a chorus of 'Baa–Baas' and other sheep-like noises.

Ronnie Lendrum, who was sub-chief to Dr Adams, had a very quick wit. One day when I was assisting him at a VD Clinic a character presented with the typical primary sore of syphilis.

Well, how do you suppose you collected this lot? queried Dr Lendrum.

Doctor, it was like this, said the patient, *You will remember that three or four weeks ago we had a very cold spell. Well, one evening I was taken sudden-like and had to pass my water while I was walking home. I think I got it* [pointing to the offending member] *frost bitten.*

Lendrum: *Quite right! Whore frost!*

However, sometimes Dr Lendrum came off second best. In an entertaining essay Dr Macdonald Critchley in his inimitable style had discoursed on 'tattooed ladies, tattooed men', pointing out that modern white people get themselves tattooed for a variety of reasons – amorous, erotic, patriotic, decorative and so on. He also commented that up to the time of World War II tattooes were of diagnostic value and that medical students were taught that tattooing in a woman was tantamount to a positive serological test for syphilis. Dr Lendrum whole-heartedly embraced this theory and was wont to comment in both sexes tattooing was positively correlated with venereal disease. One day a heavily tattooed man, a merchant seaman, was admitted to the ward. Ronnie Lendrum's eyes lit up.

How often have you been 'unlucky' my dear chap? he asked.

Three times, replied the sailor. Too good to be true, thought Ronnie, sensing an excellent opportunity for emphasising once again the relationship between tattooing and VD, when the sailor went on,

Torpedoed once in the Med, once in the Atlantic off Gib, and bombed off bloody Malta!

The months rolled past and, by 1950, my appointment as a registrar at the Western Infirmary was fast expiring. With no senior registrar vacancy in sight at 'the Western' in mid 1950, I applied for the advertised post of senior registrar to the North Regional Hospital Board, based on Inverness. Dr Adams was not amused. During his career as a senior physician he had been accustomed virtually to appointing his own staff but with the advent of the National Health Service in 1948 all appointments became the prerogative of the various Regional Hospital Boards. Dr Adams was, of course, one of my referees and wrote to the Administrative Officer, North Regional Hospital Board, Inverness painting my abilities in glowing terms but finishing the testimonial with the words:

I must confess that I learned of his application for a post in Inverness with considerable personal regret and I am entirely satisfied that your Hospital Board would be very fortunate to secure his services.

On reading this paragraph in the copy of the testimonial which he gave me I felt that the North Regional Hospital Board might well consider that they could forgo this good fortune and that they would not be a party to depriving D.K. Adams of my 'services'. However, I achieved the 'short list' and travelled by train to the Station Hotel, Inverness, where the interviews were to take place.

While the selection committee assembled, the four applicants sat together making polite conversation and three of us felt that our journey had been unnecessary on learning that the fourth applicant was already working in Inverness as a medical registrar. The selection committee comprised some members of the Hospital Board, the senior administrative medical officer, Dr Sandy Fraser, and the two consultant physicians to the Region, Dr James Ronald and Dr Tom Scott.

We were interviewed in alphabetical order. I was the third to present myself and after being asked the usual professional questions a lady member of the selection committee said 'this position entails a lot of travelling, west to Skye, east to Nairn, south to Fort William and north to Wick and Thurso. Tell me, do you know anything of our roads in the north and west of Scotland?' The questioner turned out to be Dame Flora McLeod of Dunvegan Castle in the Isle of Skye, and because of my Caithness ancestry I was able to give her a blow by blow account of motoring in the north of Scotland, enlarging on the terrors Berriedale Brae on the borders of Caithness and Sutherland used to hold for the earlier motorists of the region. Obviously pleased, the good lady said no more and I felt she regarded me with some favour compared with the poor lowland characters seated without.

After a short delay, it was announced that I had secured the position — assistant to Dr James Ronald, the tenure being for three years and the salary one thousand pounds per annum rising to one thousand two hundred pounds. I rushed to the nearest phone to inform Pat, feeling we had almost 'made it' and that consultant status and security of tenure was only a matter of time.

In late 1950, my old home *Morven* was sold and Pat, Gillian and I moved to our new home *Hawthornlea* in Midmills Road, Inverness.

The first few years in Inverness proved to be among the happiest Pat and I have experienced. *Hawthornlea* was a spacious, even gracious family home and professionally, although a senior registrar, I was consultant in everything but name. Dr James Ronald and Dr Tom Scott were both consultant physicians and Dr Aymer Wilson (Scott's assistant) and I shared the same duties as our 'chiefs' — in-patient and out-patient clinics at Wick, Thurso, Golspie, Dingwall, Nairn and Broadford, Isle of Skye and domicilliary visits as requested by the general practitioners of the region. Dr Aymer Wilson was graded 'senior medical officer' which was a step below consultant rank. Although it gave security of tenure it was generally regarded as a 'dead end' in that very few incumbents of these posts had been promoted out of them to consultant status.

The four of us, two consultants, one senior medical officer and one senior registrar, alternated in attending these outlying clinics at regular intervals, and Aymer Wilson and I took year about relieving the consultant physician at Stornoway, Outer Hebrides, for four weeks during his annual vacation. For this we received a cost of living allowance and for domicilliary visits a mileage allowance (seven 'old' pence per mile), whereas the consultants received a fee for each domicilliary visit they made up to a certain number.

We were all of a similar age, Ronald and Scott being older than me by some ten years and Aymer by four or five, and although the discrepancy in status and income performing identical work might seem unfair, for several years this system worked quite well, largely because Aymer and I felt that, provided we did the work of consultant physicians conscientiously, it would only be a matter of time before this was recognised and our posts upgraded.

But not in my time; however, that is another story ... .

Early in 1951, I applied for permission to sit the examination for membership of the Royal College of Physicians, Edinburgh, and in due course received approval of my petition from the College with a request to attend on Friday 29 June, 1951, for the written examination in Medicine.

In these days the candidate was required to sit three written papers, one on general medicine, one on therapeutics and one on a 'special subject', in my case neurology. In addition, there were two

Royal College of Physicians,
Edinburgh 2.

[12 JUN 1951

Dear Sir/Madam,

MEMBERSHIP

I am to inform you that the Council have approved your Petition and have authorised your examination by the Board of Examiners.

You are requested to appear here, 9 QUEEN STREET, EDINBURGH, on Friday, 29 .... for the written examination on Medicine (two hours) at 9.45 a.m. and on Therapeutics (two hours) at 1.45 p.m. At the beginning of the examination you will be informed as to the times and places of the clinical, practical and oral examinations.

Yours truly,

L. Jolley.

APPLICATION TO SIT FOR MEMBERSHIP OF THE
ROYAL COLLEGE OF PHYSICIANS OF
EDINBURGH

126

clinical examinations, one in general medicine and one on the 'special subject' and, finally, the *viva voce*. The 'writtens' over, I presented myself at the Western General Infirmary, Edinburgh, for the clinical examination in general medicine. This comprised a 'long case' and several 'short cases'. The 'long case' was commonly a rather unusual condition or, more often, a patient who had more than one disorder, and the candidate was given some forty minutes to take a history, examine the patient and hopefully arrive at a diagnosis. My patient was a pleasant middle aged man. He was markedly overweight and was obviously suffering from chronic bronchitis and emphysema which had conferred on him a 'barrel chest'. This rendered listening to his heart difficult partly because of respiratory squeaks and whistles but more because the barrel chest muffled and made distant the normal 'lub-dub, lub-dub' of the heart. I examined the patient from head to toe yet all I could find amiss was the very common-place respiratory ailment – surely not a long MRCP case. I was convinced that I was missing something; perspiration started to bead my brow. I had already measured respiratory excursion with a measuring tape and in desperation began to 'go over' his chest again, this time placing my outstretched hands across his chest as I asked him to 'breathe out, breathe in!', as I did so the penny dropped. Under my left hand on the right side of his chest I could just feel the regular impulse of the apex of the heart beating against the chest wall. 'Why!' I gasped, 'your heart is on the wrong side!' 'Good lad!' said the patient, 'but you better call it "dextrocardia" when they come'. 'They' were, of course, the examiners and with my confidence restored, I was able to make a reasonable fist of the rest of the examination.

The clinical examination in neurology was held at the Edinburgh Royal Infirmary, and followed a similar pattern. The inevitable 'tricky one' on this occasion was a child suffering from tuberose sclerosis. I had never personally encountered this condition before but, thanks to my 1947 edition of *Brain*, I was able to recognise the child was suffering from Bourneville's disease, an eponymous title for this uncommon disorder. Little did I imagine as I said diffidently, 'I think the child has Bourneville's disease, Sir' in a ward of the Royal Infirmary, Edinburgh, that a decade later in

Royal College of Physicians of Edinburgh

EXAMINATION FOR MEMBERSHIP

July 1951

MEDICINE

Time allowed—Two Hours

(*Answer* **three** *of the following questions*)

1. Describe the pathology of Crohn's disease (regional ileitis) and give an account of its clinical features.

2. Discuss the significance of polyuria as a symptom.

3. Discuss the diagnosis of whooping cough and give an account of its complications.

4. Discuss the aetiology and classification of the pneumonias.

NOTE: Each question must be answered separately in the appropriate book.

WRITTEN EXAMINATION IN GENERAL MEDICINE,
FOR MEMBERSHIP OF THE
ROYAL COLLEGE OF PHYSICIANS OF EDINBURGH,
1951

1961, with Professor Eadie (then my Registrar) and Professor Tyrer, I would report in the *Medical Journal of Australia* the findings in six patients suffering from tuberose sclerosis seen at the Royal Brisbane Hospital.

The final *viva voce* examination was held at the College, 9 Queen Street, Edinburgh. In keeping with the gentlemanly way in which the examination had been conducted, a rather sumptuous afternoon tea was provided for the candidates but I fear few did it justice. Who could have an appetite when one's future depended on the next hour or two.

The examination concluded about 5 p.m. and the results were to be announced at 7.30 p.m. that evening. After seeing the College Porter and asking if he would be good enough to check if my name appeared on the list of successful candidates when I phoned after 7.30, I set off for Inverness. Shortly after 7.30, I stopped at a public telephone booth in Pitlochry :

College Porter speaking.
Sutherland is my name [deep breath]... *can you tell me...*
Doctor, let me be the first to congratulate you.

Nineteen fifty-one was indeed, a 'bonus year' because some four months later Pat presented us with a son, Iain, born at Raigmore Maternity Unit on 10th October, 1951. Indeed, my cup was pretty full. Living in a pleasant home, in a countryside we loved, with a beautiful wife and daughter, a sturdy son and with, as I thought, excellent

Gillian and Iain Sutherland with their father, in winter in Inverness, 1953.

Royal College of Physicians of Edinburgh

EXAMINATION FOR MEMBERSHIP

July 1951

NEUROLOGY

Time allowed—THREE HOURS

(*Answer* ALL *questions*)

1. Describe the symptoms and treatment of Ménière's syndrome.

2. Give a brief account of Wernicke's encephalopathy.

3. What are the functions of the basal ganglia ? Describe briefly the diseases in which the pathology mainly involves these ganglia.

4. Describe the investigations you would carry out to determine the aetiology of ' fits ' which might simulate idiopathic epilepsy.

**WRITTEN EXAMINATION IN NEUROLOGY,
FOR MEMBERSHIP OF THE
ROYAL COLLEGE OF PHYSICIANS OF EDINBURGH,
1951**

JOHN AND PAT SUTHERLAND, INVERNESS, 1953

prospects for a consultant post in the region now that I had MD and MRCP qualifications, life seemed pretty good. In the 1950s Inverness was unspoiled. A country town surrounded by moor and loch, with the bulk of the Grampian Mountains looming in the south-east, Ben Wyvis in the west, the Sutherlandshire hills in the distant north, the Cromarty Firth and the Black Isle to the east, Inverness was a pleasant place in which to live and bring up one's family. The work was continuous — I was rarely off-duty except on holiday, but we were happy and counted ourselves fortunate.

Before coming to Inverness, in addition to my thesis I had published three papers and while in Inverness produced eleven more. Some reflected the type of general medicine I practised, but my strong leaning towards neurology is indicated by the fact that six of the eleven papers were on neurological subjects, and as none of my three colleagues had a penchant for neurology, I was, as Professor Mervyn Eadie has put it, 'in a sense de facto neurologist' to the northern part of Scotland. Certainly, the most significant research work I have done was performed during this period on the prevalence of multiple sclerosis in Shetland, Orkney and the mainland counties of northern Scotland, including Skye and the Outer Hebrides.

It has been said that many doctors owe a debt of gratitude to mentors who at the start of their career gave them an idea. In my case, it was DK Adams who gave me an interest in multiple sclerosis and, as indicated in my MD thesis, a feeling that the incidence and prevalence of multiple sclerosis was not uniform throughout the country. In the northern region this also appeared to be the case, in that proportionately more cases of the disease appeared to come from Caithness compared with the other counties. This possible district incidence and the fact that, although multiple sclerosis was the most common organic nervous disease in Scotland, no accurate estimate of its prevalence existed, prompted me to undertake a survey of the prevalence of the disease in the north of Scotland.

It may be recalled that in an earlier chapter Orkney and Shetland were described as being Nordic counties whose inhabitants stem from Viking ancestry whereas Sutherland is basically Highland with a Celtic heritage and Caithness is the meeting ground of both cultures. Although Orkney and Shetland are outwith the auspices of

THE BAY OF SKAILE, AND THE ORKNEY SKYLINE.

Cape Wrath

OUTER
HEBRIDES

ATLANTIC

LEWIS

OCEAN

HARRIS

NORTH
UIST

THE

MAINLAND

BENBEC
ULA

MINCH

Portree

RAASAY

SCOTLAND

SOUTH
UIST

SKYE

THE

ERISKAY

WEST

BARRA

HIGHLANDS

THE ROUTE OF

"OVER THE SEA TO SKYE"

MAP 7 , "OVER THE SEA TO SKYE"

the North Regional Board, being administered medically by the North Eastern Regional Board, it appeared of interest to include Orkney and Shetland in the survey and also to compare the prevalence in the Outer Hebrides, both equally 'closed' communities, the former Nordic, the latter being predominantly Celtic in language (Gaelic) and way of life.

I was very fortunate in the co-operation I received from the practitioners in the region, obtaining a 98.7% reply rate to my original questionnaire. Thereafter all the patients notified were personally examined by me during relieving duties in the Outer Hebrides in 1953 and during routine clinics on the mainland, while Shetland and Orkney were surveyed during a period of leave in 1954. The Advisory Committee on Medical Research (Scotland) supported me with an expense grant of three hundred pounds. To cut a long story short (it is fully reported in *Brain*, 1956. 79·635-654), the prevalence of multiple sclerosis in Shetland and Orkney (110–130 per 100,000 of the population) was twice as high as anywhere else in the survey region. It was also of interest that the prevalence of the disease in Sutherlandshire, Ross and Cromarty, mainland Inverness-shire, Nairn and the Outer Hebrides was 50 per 100,000 whereas in 'the Nordic area' of Shetland, Orkney, Caithness and Skye it was 100 per 100,000. It became apparent in later years that the prevalence rate of multiple sclerosis was higher in the Orkney and Shetland Islands than anywhere else in the world and subsequent surveys, a Swedish survey in 1962 and, notably, surveys by an American group led by Professor David Poskanzer of the Massachussets General Hospital, Boston (1970 and 1974–76) have indicated that the prevalence has remained high, and in Orkney has increased.

This was an exciting discovery and led one to believe that in the Orkney and Shetland Islands must lie the key to the aetiology of this mysterious disease. Unfortunately, despite world-wide sophisticated research, the cause and the cure of multiple sclerosis continues to elude us. It seems possible that in addition to an environmental factor, a disadvantageous genetic factor, probably associated in some way with that part of the HLA system associated with immune mechanisms, is operative. I was certainly impressed that in the 1950s the disease was more frequent in the Nordic north than in the Celtic region, correlating with the fact that counties with a high percentage of Gaelic speaking in addition to English (Sutherlandshire, Ross and Comarty, Inverness) have a lower prevalence of multiple sclerosis than Nordic (only English, non-Gaelic speaking) Orkney and Shetland. It is difficult to escape the conclusion that those derived from Nordic ancestors have a greater predisposition to multiple sclerosis than other racial groups. In the meantime, the cause of multiple sclerosis remains shrouded in the mists of these Northern Isles.

Writing of Skye and the Outer Hebrides brings to mind unique experiences which occurred in the Western Isles.

In the course of being locum tenens for the physician, Dr J.C.R. Greig, based in Stornoway on the Isle of Lewis in the Outer Hebrides, I had to visit clinics at North Uist, Benbecula, South Uist and Barra (*see Map 7*). It was off Barra that the ship *Politician*, carrying a cargo of whisky for the U.S.A., ran aground during World War II. Compton McKenzie in his hilarious novel *Whisky Galore* recounts this mishap, renaming the ship *Cabinet Minister*. After seeing a patient at her home on Barra I was asked by the husband 'Would I not be after having a dram?' On replying that I would, I was rather amazed when he said, 'Well then, I'll chust be going out to the field to get a bottle', but sure enough he returned wiping peaty-earth from an unlabelled bottle. I was about to have a dram from *The Politician*. After the crew of the ship had left, the locals 'rescued' some of the cargo and ploughed the bottles into their fields to prevent them being seized by the excise officers. Quite a number of years later some of the precious liquid remained.

On the subject of whisky, a very fine single malt named *Talisker* is distilled on the Isle of Skye and it was very pleasant after a busy clinic and a number of domicilliary visits to sit at a peat fire, sipping the pale amber liquid and listening to the stories of one or other of the local doctors.

During one of my visits to Skye, I was asked to see a patient at Flodigarry, in a house where Flora MacDonald had lived for a number of years. That evening, talk turned to Flora MacDonald and her adventures and although the story has been told many times, a good yarn and particularly a true one, is worth re-telling ......

After the disastrous defeat of his forces at Culloden on April 16, 1746, Prince Charles Edward Stuart (*Bonnie Prince Charlie*), escorted by a few faithful followers, fled to the West Highlands and eventually crossed the Minch to the Outer Hebrides, desperately attempting to avoid capture by the English and local militia and with equal desperation looking for a vessel in which he might be taken to the continent of Europe. May–June, 1746, saw the Prince, a fugitive with a price on his head and now with only two companions, wandering in South Uist, having landed from a boat on Eriskay a few miles to the south (*see Map 7*). However, there was no sanctuary in South Uist; his enemies were closing in and he would have to leave South Uist or be trapped.

Some twenty-three years previously, in 1722, Flora MacDonald had been born in South Uist at Milton but two years later her father, the local laird, died. Four years passed and then her mother remarried another MacDonald who lived at Armidale in the Isle of Skye. Flora, however, continued to live first with her brother Angus who had succeeded his father as the laird, and from 1735 with kinsfolk, the Chief of Clan Ranald and his Lady, at Ormacleit Castle in South Uist, and then in 1739 with other relatives, Sir Alexander and Lady Margaret MacDonald, at Monkstadt in the north of Skye, occasionally visiting her mother and her brother at Milton.

Lady Margaret was so impressed with Flora that she obtained permission from Flora's mother to have her education rounded off at a Ladies' Seminary in Edinburgh. Flora remained at the Seminary from 1740 to 1744 and stayed with Sir Alexander and Lady Margaret MacDonald in Edinburgh for a further year. Seventeen forty-five, however, brought news of the Duke of Cumberland's defeat at Fonteney and rumours that Prince Charles, the Young Pretender, was planning to raise the clans in rebellion. In June, 1745 the MacDonalds, accompanied by Flora, sailed from Leith to Inverness and then journeyed by horseback across Scotland to the West Coast and Skye. After remaining with her mother for a few days, Flora continued her journey back to South Uist, Milton and the Clan Ranalds. Flora MacDonald is depicted in a painting by Allan Ramsay as a slender but shapely young woman with good features and dark hair and eyes and when middle aged, James Boswell describes her as ' ... a little woman, of a genteel appearance, and uncommonly mild and well bred'.

But here we have Prince Charles Edward and Flora MacDonald in South Uist at a critical time for the former and although Clan Ranald and the MacDonalds had not joined Prince Charles' ill-fated expedition, like most Islanders and Highlanders, they had little love of the English and their sympathies were with the Prince. It appears to have been Lady Clan Ranald who suggested that Flora should return to her mother's house in Skye, taking with her the Prince disguised as her maidservant. On returning from Milton, where she had gone to acquaint her brother of the plan, Flora was arrested by a party of soldiers and next morning she was taken before their Commanding Officer. One can only imagine Flora's delight when this officer turned out to be her step-father. Although serving with the English in the local militia, his loyalties were with the Prince and he issued passports for Flora, a manservant and her Irish spinning-maid *Betty Burke* to cross to Skye in order to visit her mother.

In Benbecula the Prince became *Betty Burke* and in late June, thus attired, the Prince, Flora, Neil and a crew of five set off one evening *Over the Sea to Skye* some thirty-five miles distant. About midnight a storm arose in the treacherous Minch. In the words of the *Skye Boat Song:*

> *Loud the winds howl, loud the waves roar,*
> *Thunderclaps rend the air.*

— but eventually, with daylight the waves subsided, the mountains of Skye loomed in the distance and the open 24 foot boat rounded Vaternish Point to the accompaniment of a hail of bullets from a party of militiamen on the beach which splintered the handle of the helm, wounding the hand of the helmsman, and riddled the sails with holes. However, they crossed Loch Snizort safely, landing near Monkstadt, the home of Sir Alexander and Lady Margaret MacDonald. While the Prince hid in a cave Flora went on to the home to find that a number of militia officers were staying there as guests, Sir Alexander having declared himself for the King. The party therefore moved on to Kingsburgh some twelve miles away, the Prince still dressed as *Betty Burke*, to the house where a quarter of a century later, as mistress of the property, Flora was to relate her adventure to Dr Johnson and James Boswell.

Flora and her faithful manservant Neil accompanied the Prince to Portree and then across the two miles of sea to the island of Raasay, the laird of which had fought for the Prince at Culloden. On Raasay, Flora said good-bye to her Prince for the last time; they were never to meet again. After further adventures the Prince returned to the mainland and sailed for France in September, 1746, from Arisaig, not far distant from his original landing place.

Flora MacDonald had had her 'one hour of glorious life' and her heroism earned her a place in history. Although arrested and taken to London, she was never put on trial and regained her freedom after some twelve months. In 1750 she married Alan MacDonald and lived for some eight years at Flodigarry where she bore Alan five of her seven children. She was to have more adventures in America and on the High Seas before returning to Skye. Flora died in 1790, and is buried near Flodigarry where a monument bearing the inscription stands in her honour.

A name that will be mentioned in history, and, if courage and fidelity be virtues, mentioned with honour.

After being Flora's guest at Kingburgh in 1773, Dr Samuel Johnson next morning left a scrap of paper in his bedroom on which he had written:

Quantum cedal virtutibus aurum.

[With virtue weighed what worthless trash is gold.]

There is no need to say more.

A Far Off Sunlit Place

In the 1950s, there was a pleasant hotel at Flodigarry much frequented by southern visitors during the summer months. There was also a doctor, a fellow graduate of Glasgow University, but quite elderly when I knew him and something of a worthy. On one occasion a lady guest from the hotel consulted him when an intractable skin condition flared up while she was on holiday. The doctor made up a mixture for her to be taken orally (in these days many country doctors had their own dispensaries), and to the dear lady's delight the skin condition, which had resisted the best efforts of London dermatologists, yielded to this treatment. Sometime after her return south she experienced a further flare up. She wrote the good doctor asking for the prescription of the medicine he had given her but received no reply; she wrote again an imploring letter but to no avail. In some desperation she wrote to the manager of the hotel asking him to intercede. 'Why on earth, doctor, will you not send the poor lady a prescription?' asked the manager one day. 'Well now, 'tis like this' replied the doctor, 'I know the Latin for sulphur but I'm "puggered" if I know the Latin for treacle!' (In its day 'sulphur and treacle' was a homely remedy for a host of ills.)

No mention of the Outer Hebrides would be complete without referring to the MacBrayne's steamships which plied between the mainland and the Western Isles. It was said 'God made the Hebrides but MacBrayne built the piers.' The Captain of one of those ships was nicknamed *Squeaky* because of his rather high pitched voice — we will name him Captain MacFarlane — I cannot recall his correct surname. One day during the second World War a Rear Admiral was taking passage with him *en route* to inspect some installation or other in the Outer Hebrides and Captain MacFarlane courteously invited the Admiral on to his bridge. As the little vessel was heading across the Minch towards Barra the Admiral said 'Captain MacFarlane, I wonder if I could see your chart of these waters?' 'Of course,' replied Captain MacFarlane, who had not looked at 'a chart of these waters' for years and squeaked to the Mate, 'Dougie, be you a good lad now and find the Admiral the chart.' After some considerable time Dougie reappeared and proffered the Admiral a rather crumpled, dusty chart with still a few cobwebs adhering to it, which he had found in the wheelhouse. The Admiral spread out the chart and invited Captain MacFarlane to indicate his ship's position on it. 'My God! MacFarlane!' cried the Admiral, 'We are standing into a minefield.' 'Well, well, now,' squeaked the Captain looking at the marks on the chart at which the Admiral's finger was tremulously pointing, 'if these are what you think they are it is a very bad thing that will be after happening to us this day, but if it is what I think they are we will be right enough'. 'What do you think the marks indicate then, Captain MacFarlane?' 'Flyshit', quoth the Captain.

The years in the northern region of Scotland passed quickly. I enjoyed my work and Pat and I had a wide circle of friends. However, by 1955, my three years contract had long expired and I had been retained for the past two years on an annual reappointment basis. I was, therefore, particularly disappointed to learn that at a meeting on staffing requirements in the Northern Region, Dr Ronald, my superior, had not supported the creation of further consultant posts in medicine in the region. It, therefore, seemed imperative that I obtain another teaching hospital appointment as a step to achieving a consultant post outwith the Northern Region. I applied for and was successful in obtaining a position as senior registrar to Dr Duthie at Aberdeen Royal Infirmary, and it was with very mixed feelings that we moved to Aberdeen in 1955. Both Dr Duthie and Dr Tom Morgan, his subchief who had a special interest in neurology, were pleasant to work with and the work itself was less arduous and carried much less responsibility than I had become accustomed to in Inverness.

A post of consultant physician to the Western Infirmary, Glasgow, was advertised and I was thrilled to achieve the short list of five candidates and to be invited to appear before the selection committee. Dr D.K. Adams who was still on the staff of the Western Infirmary, strongly supported my application. Dr Duthie virtually guaranteed me the job. Dr James Ronald of Inverness was equally supportive writing, *inter alia,*

... during his spell in Inverness he carried out extensive duties with conspicuous success, undertaking the care of patients in the wards and conducting out-patient clinics both in Inverness and throughout the Region. He is a very hard worker with a keen incisive brain whose observations are meticulously accurate, and who has a happy knack of penetrating rapidly to the essentials of the problem. He has a particular bent towards research work and has published numerous papers ...

In the event, the short list narrowed to two but I lost, I believe, on the casting vote of the Chairman of the selection committee, Professor Wayne, Professor of Medicine, University of Glasgow.

I have no hard feelings about this. I had 'a win' at Inverness and Aberdeen, but 'a loss' at Glasgow. I read recently a very good article 'How to achieve success in Medicine'. The author emphasized that 'patronage of the undeserving is curtailed in the National Health Service by appointment committees but influence is still important'. He went on —

... supportive colleagues are invaluable all the way up the ladder to success ... Being on the power network is in a person's interests ...

These comments bear the hallmark of truth and experience. For my own part, I have encountered in the past three types of senior doctors. There are a few like D.K. Adams, J.B. Gaylor and Douglas McAlpine who actively do their best to promote the career of younger colleagues. The majority adopt a passive role. A few, for some reason or another, are positively obstructive.

However, in March, 1956, I applied for a post of consultant physician at Derby, and about the same time, lying in bed one Saturday night glancing through the *British Medical Journal*, my eye caught a notice. I nudged Pat who was deeply engrossed in a book. 'How would you like to go to Australia?' She replied absently, without lifting her eyes from the print, 'Oh, alright, provided there are no snakes or "creepy-crawlies".'

I duly sent off an application for the post of Senior Lecturer in Medicine, University of Queensland, Australia, and within a few days of each other I was informed I had been short listed for the Derby appointment and the Queensland one. I then received a telephone call from Dr Justin O'Reilly, a Queenslander who was in Britain and had been asked to represent the University of Queensland in the matter of my application, and could he come to Aberdeen to interview me?

Justin O'Reilly was a very likeable chap and I later came to know him well as a pathologist working with Dr John Tonge. I met him at Aberdeen Station and took him to our bungalow in Kingshill Road, where he sat at the fire with my son, Iain, on his knee running a 'Dinky' car up and down the lapels of the good doctor's jacket. It was a very informal affair and I suspect only to ensure we were house trained. At any rate, within a few days a cable arrived offering me the position and requesting an immediate reply.

The date of the interview at Derby was a month ahead and after a very short deliberation and discussion with Pat we decided on Australia for a trial period of three years – to ensure that there were no snakes or 'creepy crawlies'. A cable was sent to Australia accepting the position and a letter to Derby withdrawing my name from the short list – I liked that! Shortly afterwards I received a letter dated May 21, 1956, under the signature of C. Page Hanify, Registrar, University of Queensland, confirming my appointment 'to the position of Senior Lecturer (Clinical) in Medicine'.

I was certainly disappointed at not achieving the Western Infirmary position and returning to my *alma mater* but not more so than my old chief, mentor and friend, Dr D.K. Adams, who wrote a very touching letter after we had said farewell to him on leaving Scotland for Australia:

My Dear John,

I need hardly say how great was my personal pleasure at seeing you again and my very great regret at the remote chance of our meeting again.

It would have warmed your heart to hear of the regret in the Western that you were not returning to the staff.

The meeting I had to attend and seeing the way you were treated after all your high endeavours and first class performance made me feel spiritually ill!

Taking a broader view, all may be for the best. You have gained professional freedom ... the teaching opportunities alone that now lie ahead would fire anyone's ambition and yours never really needed firing.

I need hardly add you take with you all our warmest wishes for health, success and happiness ... and don't forget your real friends of whom you have many in the Glasgow School of Medicine.

Yours ever,
(**Signed**) *Douglas K. Adams.*

On 10th October, 1956, we sailed on the P and O liner *Oronsay* from Southampton, bound for Australia. Apart from the first Suez crisis breaking out, necessitating a long haul around the Cape and then down the roaring forties to Fremantle, we were voyaging *West over Sea* in the spirit of our Nordic forebears!

PART II

Far off in sunlit places, sad are the Scottish faces,
Yearning to feel the kiss of sweet Scottish rain.
Where tropic skies are beaming, love sets the heart
    a dreaming,
Longing and dreaming for the homeland again.

Scotland the Brave
Clifford Hanley

A FAR OFF SUNLIT PLACE

QUEENSLAND 1956-1959

ronsay arrived in Fremantle in late October, 1956 and after a dash across the Great Australian Bight at considerably more than economical speed reached Melbourne on Melbourne Cup Day. A day or so later we disembarked at Sydney. After four cool rather dreary weeks at sea it was very pleasant to enjoy Western Australian sunshine in Kings Park, Perth. In Melbourne not only was the Melbourne Cup being run but the city was gaily decorated for the Olympic Games — rather a splendid welcome! As indeed was the experience of being shown something of Melbourne by a lady who came aboard *Oronsay* introducing herself as the Aunt of one Kenneth Jamieson, a neurosurgeon at the then Brisbane General Hospital, who had asked her to 'look us up' when *Oronsay* docked at Melbourne.

Australians certainly take 'new chums' under their wing. In addition to this pleasant gesture from a future colleague there was the heart warming experience of a Melbourne taxi driver who returned several times to the ship in an attempt to return my wallet which I had dropped in his cab, and the kindness of the sleeping car attendant who looked after us on the train journey from Sydney to Brisbane. As the train drew into the Interstate Station, Brisbane, Professor John Tyrer was waiting on the platform to welcome us and to escort us to the Bellevue Hotel, where he had arranged our

Professor John Tyrer CBE
Photo, circa 1982

accommodation. The formalities of arrival over, John asked me would I like a pre-lunch drink. I clearly recall my first impressions ... because I had grown up with a mental picture of middle aged rather austere professors of medicine, my initial reaction was 'What a young professor!' (John Tyrer is, indeed some months younger than I.) The second impression, on a seven ounce glass of beer being placed before a man accustomed to a pint tankard, was 'what a small beer!'

We had arrived in Brisbane where we were to lead such a happy life for so many years. Over these years momentous events were to follow one after another on the world stage — the election of General de Gaulle as Prime Minister of France (1958). the election of Mr John Kennedy as the 35th President of the United States (1961) and his subsequent assassination (1963); the death of Sir Winston Churchill (1965). the first human heart transplant operation by Dr Christian Barnard (1967); Armstrong and Aldren of the USA, the first humans to land on the moon (1969). Mr Whitlam, the first Labour Prime Minister of Australia in a quarter of a century (1972) and the dismissal of his government by the Governor General, Sir John Kerr (1975); Mrs Margaret Thatcher, the first woman to be Prime Minister of Britain

(1979) – and so on – the conflicts in the Middle East, the Vietnam war to the British campaign against Argentinian forces in the Falklands.

But back in 1956, in Brisbane, the Sutherlands had to find permanent accommodation. The Bellevue Hotel was rapidly reducing us to penury and Pat was fortunate in finding more suitable accommodation in New Farm, where the friendly hospitality of Elsie and Tom Dunstan at *Coolden* was to help us adjust to an environment so different from the one we had left. Over the years we have not lost contact with *Coolden* and continue to hold Elsie Dunstan in the highest esteem.

From *Coolden* Pat and the children set out on many house hunting expeditions in the tropical heat and humidity of a Brisbane November, until at last *The Sheiling*, Harts Road, Indooroopilly, was discovered and we took up residence there just before Christmas, 1956.

The Sheiling, Harts Road, Indooroopilly, Brisbane. Photo, circa 1957.

Because the final examinations in Medicine were imminent, I started work within a day or two of arriving in Brisbane. One of my first duties was to assess patients notified to the Department of Medicine as being suitable for examination purposes and to make notes of the salient features of each case. I well remember dragging myself along in the wake of Dr Herbert Copeman, then registrar to Professor Tyrer, as he conducted me from ward to ward of the Brisbane General Hospital. My complaints of heat exhaustion, dehydration and anuria fell on deaf ears! Elsewhere Professor Mervyn Eadie has written 'In late 1956 a quick moving, tall, dark-haired Scot ... began to appear around the wards of the then Brisbane General Hospital'. 'Quick moving!' I am jolly sure this description did not apply to me in November, 1956, as I crawled from the oasis of one ward to another.

Professor John Howard Tyrer graduated from Sydney University in 1942, and was appointed to the University of Queensland as its first full-time Professor of Medicine in 1954. Prior to John's appointment Sir Alexander Murphy and later Sir Ellis Murphy had served as half-time Professors of Medicine at the Brisbane General Hospital in addition to the responsibilities of their extensive private practices. The Brisbane General Hospital had long been accustomed to providing patient care and treatment and one sensed within the administration of the hospital some embarrassment that now, as a teaching hospital, the further obligations of teaching and research had also to be fulfilled. Prior to the erection of the Tooth Lecture Theatre and Research Laboratories the only research facility available was an area in Ward 4C which John Tyrer had succeeded in having walled off for this purpose. Teaching was conducted either at the bedside or in a small dark lecture theatre termed 'the dungeon'.

It was, however, exciting being 'in' at the beginning, as it were. In 1954 Professor Tyrer had a daunting task ahead of him. In 1955 he was joined by Dr Alfred William Steinbeck as Reader so that with my arrival, in 1956, John had an academic staff of three, including himself.

A measure of how well Professor Tyrer succeeded in meeting the challenge is the fact that on his retirement three decades later there were fifteen full-time academic staff members including

Dr Kenneth Jamieson and daughter.

Professor Brian Emmerson at the Princess Alexandra Hospital, Professor L.W. Powell and Professor M.J. Eadie at the Royal Brisbane Hospital and Professor R.D. Gordon at Greenslopes Repatriation Hospital. The staff also included three senior Research Fellows together with other medical and research personnel, and there is also a sub-department at the Mater Misericordiae Hospital.

Our medical work comprised the care of in-patients in Ward 4C, out-patient clinics (medical, neurological and endocrine – Dr Steinbeck) and interunit consultations. Dr Kenneth Grant Jamieson in 1955 had been appointed the Royal Brisbane Hospital's first neurosurgeon and his presence attracted an increasing number of neurosurgical and neurological patients. As at that time John Tyrer and I were the only hospital staff members with specialised neurological training, we had a rapidly expanding in-patient and out-patient neurological practice, in addition to general medicine, and close professional and personal links were forged with Dr Jamieson.

On one occasion Dr Jamieson was invited to see a patient in Ward 4C in consultation. I cannot recall the symptomatology but the diagnosis had eluded us. Neither John nor I were present when Kenneth Jamieson examined the patient but shortly afterwards John Tyrer rushed into my office pointing to Ken's neatly written entry 'GOK.KGJ' in the case record and, fearing we had missed a perfectly obvious diagnosis, almost whispered, 'What *is* 'GOK'?' I was equally nonplussed but, not being a professor, less worried and in due course waylaid our neurosurgical colleague. 'GOK', said Ken, 'Why, God Only Knows!'

I found my Scottish brogue something of a handicap. When lecturing to a new batch of students, they would sit in stunned disbelief for a week or two. Thereafter, with a lessening of dialectal difficulties and with some understanding of the language, their level of consciousness steadily improved. Indeed, I can almost detect a trace of a Scottish accent in a few of my former students and registrars – a relic of our previous association.

Another example: shortly after my arrival I was taking a very bright lady student over the 'long case' of her final clinical examination. I was being my usual gentle self (particularly with a good looking young lady!) when she burst into tears crying 'Dr Sutherland! I cannot understand one word you say.'

During these early years there was little time or opportunity for organised research and our published work was in the main based on clinical experiences. During the first year or two I was promoted laterally to Senior Lecturer in Materia Medica and Therapeutics, thus making way for Dr Martyn Lloyd from England to be appointed Senior Lecturer in Medicine. Out of this dalliance with therapeutics emerged 'Antibiotics and diuretics' (*Ann. General Practice.* 3: 123-127: 1958). 'Chlorothiazide in the treatment of toxaemia of pregnancy' (*Proceedings of International Symposium on Chlorothiazide and Other Diuretics, Hong Kong, 1958*). 'A report of some therapeutic trials' (*Med. J. Australia,* 2, 470-473: 1959) – and a trip to Hong Kong courtesy of Merck Sharp and Dohme, while I preserved my neurological integrity with 'Familial spastic paraplegia' (*Lancet.* 2. 169-170. 1957).

Aside from Medicine and Neurology, John Tyrer and I had

two other things in common, Sherlock Holmes and horse riding. It seems probable that our training in the Oslerian tradition of observation and the assessment of evidence was the reason we held Sherlock Holmes in high regard. This art, or discipline of observation and deduction, had been brought to a pinnacle of perfection by Dr Joseph Bell, Surgeon to the Royal Infirmary, Edinburgh, and it was on his old teacher that Dr (later Sir) Arthur Conan Doyle based the technique of the great detective. Neurology lends itself to this traditional system and in 1967, eighty years after Sherlock first appeared in *A Study in Scarlet* (1887), Tyrer and I published our own modest 'Whodunnit' entitled *Exercises in Neurological Diagnosis.* This little volume enjoyed some success, running to three English editions (the third in 1981, with Professor Eadie as a co-author) and an Italian edition. It was based on the premise that –

> *The doctor reviewing the signs and symptoms which guide him to a diagnosis of his patient's malady, has much in common with the detective who studies clues which guide him to a solution of the crime he investigates.* [Douglas Guthrie]

We set out 'the clues', allowed the reader to reach his solution and then supplied the diagnosis – and, hopefully, some advice!

For a number of years John Tyrer and I went horse riding each Saturday morning. In the middle and late 1950s, the Brisbane suburbs of Kenmore and Pullenvale were largely undeveloped and there were many quiet roads and pathways along which to ride without the interruption of motor vehicles passing by. The horses were originally the property of the late Mr John Nunn who ran a riding school in the district and whose animals were maintained in excellent condition. After John discontinued riding, Gillian and I and later Iain went to the riding school each Sunday afternoon. By this time I owned an Australian stock horse, *Bess*, which John Nunn looked after for me. Enjoyable afternoons were spent indulging in timed cross-country events, bending races and the like and polocross or, more accurately, a form of polocross. *Bess* was about ten years old and in earlier years had traversed many a stock route. She was very sure-footed and courageous but even a sure-footed stock horse can have mishaps. During one bending race she slipped at the top marker — one moment I was in the saddle, the next on the ground gazing into one large brown eye which was regarding me rather coldly. Another time she lost her footing in a creek and as she went down on her knees I went over her head much to the delight of John Nunn, Gillian and Iain. However, in due course Pat put her foot down and my riding days came to an end.

In 1956 or 1957, I heard of a Resident Medical Officer who had correctly diagnosed a patient as suffering from Creutzfeldt — Jakob disease (subacute spongiform encephalopathy) in the Casualty Department of the hospital — of all places! This is a rare disorder occurring in about one in a million of the population and for a young RMO to have heard of it, far less diagnose the disease, was unusual. As 1957 advanced into 1958, a medical registrar, although not on the University staff at that time, would often accompany me on inter-unit consultations and showed a very considerable knowledge of and interest in neurology. The two doctors were the one and the same, Mervyn John Eadie, of whom more anon.

Professor Tyrer has written elsewhere —

Dr Sutherland, long the target as favourite consultant of the Brisbane Hospital neurosurgeons was lured into private practice.

Ken Jamieson, the first neurosurgeon to the hospital and I had, indeed, become close personal friends and, at a Christmas party held by Dr Keith Mowatt in 1958, he suggested that I should consider joining him in private practice at Selby House, Wickham Terrace, Brisbane, where he had rooms in association with Dr Howard Tait. This proposal necessitated a lot of consideration and discussion. I asked the opinion of Dr David Henderson, a physician to Brisbane General Hospital, and in private practice on Wickham Terrace, and who proved to be a very true friend. I also consulted Sir Alexander Murphy, the doyen of the medical profession in Queensland, who gave me his blessing and the excellent advice that I must restrict my private practice to purely neurological problems. Indeed, the first private patient I saw was referred to me by Sir Alexander.

The die was cast when it became apparent that my application would be considered for the position of neurologist to the Brisbane General Hospital, and Brisbane Children's Hospital. I resigned from the University in October, 1959, and on 22nd December, 1959, was appointed 'part-time Senior Neurologist on the staff of the Brisbane Hospital' and, on 23rd December, as Senior Neurologist to the Children's Hospital. My long held ambition to be a consultant neurologist to a teaching hospital was fulfilled.

Happily, my association with the University of Queensland was not severed. Commencing in December, 1959, I became a 'part-time Research Associate in Neurology within the University Department of Medicine', later a part-time Lecturer and Research Associate, followed by part-time Lecturer and Research Consultant in Neurology, and in May, 1969, the Senate of the University appointed me Honorary Reader in Neurology. I would like to think that this link between the University Department of Medicine and

'... the good relations which existed between the two Departments'.
JMS (left) with Professor John Tyrer in jovial mood.

what was to become the Department of Neurology and Neurosurgery of the Royal Brisbane Hospital has been to the advantage of both. Certainly, the amount of original work accomplished by members of the Department of Neurology subsequent to 1959 could not have been performed in the absence of the good relations and liaison which existed between the two departments. In due course Dr Eadie became a part-time Research Fellow of the University Department of Medicine while Professor Tyrer became an Honorary Neurologist to the Hospital Department of Neurology and Neurosurgery.

The reputation of a department and its members must rest not only on clinical expertise but also on —

> ... *originality, teaching by word of mouth, teaching by the printed page* ... [W.J. Mayo]

The University attachment which the Department of Neurology enjoyed made possible the reputation it was to achieve in the years ahead. A similar association between the University and other hospital departments could only be to the advantage of Medicine in Queensland, to the Hospital, and to the University.

THE DEPARTMENT OF NEUROLOGY AND NEUROSURGERY
The Royal Brisbane Hospital
1959-1973

In 1967 the names of the Brisbane Children's Hospital and the Brisbane Hospital (or the Brisbane General Hospital), were officially changed to the Royal Children's Hospital and the Royal Brisbane Hospital, respectively. In this chapter the new names will be used throughout.

With my new appointments I became, in 1959, the first visiting neurologist to be appointed to the Royal Brisbane Hospital and the Royal Children's Hospital and the only neurologist in private practice in Queensland to restrict his practice solely to neurology. In Australia, as in Britain, diagnostic neurology fell largely within the ambit of general medicine and trained neurologists of the calibre of Sir Kenneth Noad and Dr E Graeme Robertson had been appointed to their hospitals as physicians. It was not until 1944, for example, that Dr Graeme Robertson was appointed neurologist to the Royal Melbourne Hospital. And so it was in Brisbane : both Sir Ellis Murphy and Dr Peter Landy, trained neurologists, practised as physicians and neurologists.

In neurosurgery the position was very similar. Prior to World War II, there were very few departments of neurosurgery in the teaching hospitals of Britain and the Commonwealth and equally few men who would be regarded as neurosurgeons in the modern sense of the word. Sir William Macewen of Glasgow (1848–1924) and Sir Victor Horsley of London (1857–1916) were the great pioneers of neurosurgery but it is to the third member of the hagiolatry, Harvey Cushing, of Harvard and later Yale, U.S.A. (1869–1939) that credit belongs for influencing not only American but also British and Australian doctors to establish outstanding departments of neurosurgery in their teaching hospitals — men such as Sir Hugh Cairns, first at the London Hospital and later at Oxford, Sir Geoffrey Jefferson at Manchester and Sir Norman Dott at Edinburgh. In Australia, similar neurosurgical units were set up in Sydney (R.A. Money, Gilbert Phillips, Sir Douglas Miller), Melbourne (A.E. Coates, H.C. Trumble, F.P. Morgan and A. Schuller), and Adelaide (Sir Leonard Lindon).

In Brisbane, prior to 1955, there were no neurosurgical appointments but the Professor of Surgery (Neville Sutton) and Dr A.E. Lee, both general surgeons, were well versed in neurosurgical procedures and techniques. However, in 1955, the post of Visiting Neurosurgeon at the Royal Brisbane Hospital was established. Dr Kenneth Grant Jamieson was the first neurosurgeon to be appointed to this position.

Dr Jamieson ('Ken') qualified in 1948 from the University of Melbourne after an illustrious undergraduate career in which he had passed each year with honours and rowed both for his College (Ormond) and for the University. He was appointed junior Resident Medical Officer (RMO) to the Royal Melbourne Hospital, and retained his affiliation with that hospital until he came to Brisbane. His training at the Royal Melbourne in neurology and neurosurgery was done under the auspices and guidance of Dr E. Graeme Robertson, Mr Reginald Hooper, Mr H.C. Trumble and Mr K.C. Bradley (Melbourne retains the British custom of addressing surgeons as 'Mr' : Brisbane has followed the American 'Dr'). After a locum-tenency as neurosurgeon at the Royal Perth Hospital (April–July, 1955), Ken took up his appointment in Brisbane and with his wife, Margaret, and young family settled in Windermere Road, Ascot.

Several other relevant events occurred about this time. Dr Peter Tod, a Sydney graduate of 1942, was appointed Director of Diagnostic Radiology at the Royal Brisbane Hospital. Prior to coming to Brisbane Peter had gained a great deal of neuroradiological

Dr Peter Tod,
of Brisbane.

Photo, c. 1961

Dr Howard Tait, consultant psychiatrist, who established
electroencephalography at the Royal Brisbane Hospital.

experience in Sydney and, in 1962, was to become Neuroradiologist to the Royal Brisbane Hospital. The second event was the appointment, in 1954, of John Tyrer to the Chair of Medicine, University of Queensland and as a Senior Physician to the Royal Brisbane Hospital. Prior to coming to Brisbane John had spent a year (1953) working as Honorary Clinical Assistant at Lord Brain's Neurological Unit at the London Hospital, and on joining the Royal Brisbane Hospital had started a Neurology Clinic. Finally, a Queensland graduate of 1949, a psychiatrist, returned from overseas in 1955, after studying electroencephalography at the Neurological Institute, Montreal, and in London. He was Dr Howard Tait, who was to establish electroencephalography at the Royal Brisbane Hospital, and with Dr Jamieson was to share private practice facilities, including electroencephalography, at Selby House, 87 Wickham Terrace.

The original building, dating from 1866, of the Brisbane General Hospital, later to be the Royal Brisbane Hospital. Photo, c. 1960.

Thus, when Dr Jamieson commenced working at the Royal Brisbane Hospital he had the nucleus of his team—a neurologist in Professor Tyrer, a neuroradiologist in Dr Tod and an electroencephalographer in Dr Tait. He was soon to incorporate a highly trained anaesthetist into his neurosurgical group. Dr Tess O'Rourke-Brophy (now Professor Cramond) qualified from the University of Queensland in 1951, and after overseas training joined the staff of the Royal Brisbane Hospital as visiting anaesthetist in 1957. Ken Jamieson was anxious to incorporate a specialised anaesthetist in his team and the expertise of Dr Brophy well suited her for this role.

Dr Mervyn Eadie in 1955.

The period 1956 to 1960 was for Dr Jamieson a period of organisation, re-cruitment of colleagues to his department and of securing adequate facilities. I joined the Visiting Staff as Senior Neurologist in 1959, with Dr M.J. Eadie as my registrar, and in 1960 the new Depart-ment of Neurosurgery was opened, a department whose facilities we shared with the neurosurgeons, including a quota of beds. In 1961, Dr M.J. Eadie was the second Neurologist to be appointed to the Royal Brisbane Hospital and Royal Children's Hospital and in 1962 we were joined by Dr J.D.N. Yelland, the second Neurosurgeon to be appointed. In 1962, because of the close relationship which existed between Neurology and Neurosurgery and the staff members of the two departments, with the blessing of Dr A.D.D. Pye, the Medical Superintendent of the Royal Brisbane Hospital, the two departments merged becoming the Department of Neurology and Neurosurgery, the Royal Brisbane Hospital.

The new Unit, opened in 1960, comprised Wards 2B and 4B, redesigned to include two operating theatres, an X-ray department and an acute post operative ward (15 beds, 3 cots) and the Neurosurgical office with, across the corridor, the investigatory—

convalescent ward (thirty-six beds), EEG department and Neurology office.

In the ensuing years the Department of Neurology and Neuro-surgery became firmly established. For this, much credit belongs to colleagues who joined us, some to stay, others to move on to other fields or to other hospitals. Particular reference should be made to those who were at one time registrars in the Neurology Unit, because it is on one's first lieutenant that most of the work and a great deal of responsibility devolves. After Dr (now Professor) M.J. Eadie came Dr D.A. Bowman, an English girl, and then in succession Dr R. Davies, Dr T.G. Eckert, Dr P.R. Mann, Dr V.E. Edwards, Dr D.B. Appleton, Dr J.M. Bradfield, Dr J.C. Burke and Dr D.G. Banney. It is a matter of particular pleasure and satisfaction that, with the exception of Drs Dorothy Bowman, Davies and Eckert, in addition to Professor Eadie the others became consultant neurologists. On the surgical side of the Department at least four neurosurgical registrars have become neurosurgeons, three (Dr G.S. Merry, Dr J.A. Smith and Dr G.C. Stuart) being at present honoured members of the Department of Neurosurgery, the Royal Brisbane Hospital, and Royal Children's Hospital.

But of my three colleagues, Mervyn Eadie, Kenneth Jamieson and John Yelland, I must write a little more.

M. J. EADIE

Mervyn John Eadie ('Merv') is of Scottish stock, the grandson of a Girvan family. Girvan is in Ayrshire and is situated on the mainland just across the Firth of Clyde from the Isle of Arran (*see Map 4*). Merv was born on 9th October, 1932 and was educated at Brisbane Grammar School and the University of Queensland, graduating with honours in 1955. He was appointed RMO to the Royal Brisbane Hospital in 1956, and has remained on the staff of the hospital ever since, including a period as Neurology Registrar (1959–60), and in 1961 was the second Visiting Neurologist to be appointed to the Royal Brisbane and Royal Children's Hospitals.

His academic record speaks for itself. He passed the examination for membership of the Royal Australian College of Physicians in 1959, and was elevated to the Fellowship in 1968. While still a registrar in neurology he did much of the work which led to his thesis 'Studies on Parkinsonism and its alimentary manifestations' for which, in 1962, he was awarded the MD of Queensland University. Eight years later, in 1969, he achieved a second doctorate (PhD) for his thesis on 'Clinical and histochemical studies on giddiness mechanisms'. In 1961, Mervyn joined with me in private practice, initially at Selby House, Wickham Terrace, until, in 1964, we moved, with Ken Jamieson, John Yelland and Howard Tait, to *Ladhope*.

Professor Mervyn Eadie, Professor of Neurology and Neuropharmacology in the University of Queensland. Photo, 1988.

In 1962 M.J. Eadie became a part-time Research Fellow, University of Queensland and while continuing in hospital and private practice became, in succession, part-time Lecturer, part-time Reader and half-time Reader in Neurology and Neuropharmacology. In 1977, he was appointed to a Personal Chair as Professor of Clinical Neurology and Neuropharmacology, University of Queensland.

His early promise has thus been more than fulfilled. Combined with an extremely high intelligence he has the energy and drive to undertake and complete quickly an immense amount of work. In proposing Mervyn for election to the Fellowship of the Royal College of Physicians, Edinburgh, I wrote in 1984 that —

I was informed many years ago [actually by Dr D.K. Adams] *that after Professor Carl Browning had been appointed to his department, Sir Robert Muir (Professor of Pathology, University of Glasgow and the Western*

Infirmary, Glasgow) said of his colleague something to this effect 'I had been associated with him for only a short time when I realised I was in the presence of an intellect far superior to my own!' While in no way aspiring to the status of the great pathologist, my feelings regarding Professor Eadie would be similar to those expressed by Sir Robert.

It was gratifying to have him duly elected to my 'old' College.

Mervyn is happily married to Margaret, the daughter of the late Mr J.C. Slaughter, one time Town Clerk of Brisbane. They have a son, a doctor, and two daughters. Mervyn Eadie and I have been associated for some thirty years. We have been colleagues in the hospital which brought our paths together; we have been associated in University medical practice and teaching; we have collaborated in writing numerous papers and several books. Professor Eadie has been and continues to be a true friend and colleague.

DR KENNETH G. JAMIESON

'Ken was a family man.'

K. G. JAMIESON

I have already mentioned something of Ken's background. Born on January 2nd, 1925, in Melbourne, he was educated at Scotch College, Melbourne and at Melbourne University, graduating in medicine in 1948, and proceeding to MS in 1954. His further academic achievements comprised FRACS (1963), FACS (1970) by election, and MD (Melbourne) and DS (Queensland) by theses.

Combined with his academic achievements, Ken Jamieson was an astute diagnostician, a dextrous and innovative surgeon and a superb organiser. He was President of the Neurosurgical Society of Australia from 1971–73, and was on the Council of the Royal Australasian College of Surgeons. His research work was mainly in the field of head injuries, the prevention of road accidents, and the operative treatment of vertebro-basilar aneurysms and pineal tumours.

Apart from professional interests in common, Ken and I were compatible companions and became close friends. He used to visit my rooms at *Ladhope* each morning and because I was some six years his senior and in view of our Scottish ancestry his invariable query to my secretary was 'Is the Laird and Master in?'

Ken was a family man and enjoyed a happy home life with Margaret and their six children. It was invariably a pleasure to visit them and, just as Ken was an excellent speaker and lecturer, he was an amusing raconteur at the dinner table – and a generous host. Those of us who were his friends and colleagues were devastated by his death at the age of fifty-one on January 28th, 1976.

J.D.N. YELLAND

John Douglas Newman Yelland was born on 11 August 1928 and was educated at Charters Towers and at the University of Queensland, graduating MB BS in 1951, and eleven years later, in 1962, was the second neurosurgeon to be appointed to the Royal Brisbane Hospital, the Royal Children's Hospital and Princess Alexandra Hospital. In the interim he had been to England where he had been highly successful in two fields of endeavour. He had successfully won the hand of Margaret, a graduate in Medicine of Durham University, and had achieved the Fellowship of the Royal College of Surgeons of England at his first attempt.

After returning to Brisbane in 1958 and joining the staff of the Department of Neurology and Neurosurgery, John Yelland proved himself a sound diagnostician, a highly competent surgeon and a loyal supportive colleague. Unperturbable and with a rather reserved disposition, he was a quiet achiever, no-one could have worked with a more industrious and loyal colleague. John Yelland and Kenneth Jamieson complemented each other and were a perfect team. Since Ken's death John, with Dr Glen Merry, Dr Jim Smith and Dr Gordon Stuart, has maintained the reputation of the Department at the Royal Brisbane and Royal Children's Hospitals which Ken and he worked so hard to establish. Professor Eric Saint, one-time Dean of the Faculty of Medicine, wrote of these early years of the Department —

> ... *A vigorous team was established. The work load was heavy, taxing the stamina of even the most vigorous of men.*

This remains true of the Neurosurgical Department today, but was even more so of the Department in the early 1960s.

One of Dr Yelland's main interests has been the study of the outcome of treatment of hydrocephalus of infancy and childhood, with particular reference to intellectual and motor development, educational needs and achievements. This work has been done in association with Mrs Thelma McConnel, a highly regarded clinical psychologist and teacher within the Department of Child Health at the Royal Children's Hospital and with Dr D.B. Appleton, paediatric neurologist. At one time in my career I felt rather helpless dealing with hydrocephalic children. John Yelland showed me by his results over many years that much can be achieved.

Margaret and John Yelland have five children, three of whom are doctors.

Dr John Yelland (left) with Patricia and John Sutherland.
Toowoomba, August 1986.

"WE BAND OF BROTHERS"

Left to Right: Dr (later Professor) Mervyn Eadie; Dr K.G. Jamieson; Dr J.D.N. Yelland. Dr J.M. Sutherland. Photo, 1965.

In the early years of the Department we were, indeed, ' ... a happy few, we band of brothers' and I count myself fortunate in having walked along some of life's way with Kenneth Jamieson, John Yelland and Mervyn Eadie.

As a department our aim was to follow the customary tradition of a teaching hospital in regard to Practice, Education and Research.

Practice

Annual Reports of the work of the department were published and sent to other neurological–neurosurgical departments in Australia and overseas. In 1967, the Centenary Year of the Royal Brisbane Hospital, the Report reviewed the activities of the department over the preceding five years (from its inception in 1962 to the end of 1966). I thought it might be of historical interest to review some of the data presented in that Report.

During these years the Department received patients from the Princess Alexandra Hospital (neurosurgeon, Dr Yelland), from Chermside (now Prince Charles) Hospital, from Base Hospitals throughout the State and from New Guinea some 1500 miles to the north.

The staff of the Department in 1967 is shown in Table 1. (*See Appendices*).

The number of patients attending the Neurology and Neurosurgical out-patient clinics at the Royal Brisbane Hospital is shown in Table 2, a total of 1926 new neurology cases and 395 new neurosurgical cases being seen. At the Royal Children's Hospital two neurological clinics were held each week. The attendances at the neurology clinic over the five year period numbered 3,111 children. No figures are available for paediatric neurosurgical out-patients.

For children requiring in-patient neurological investigation or treatment, a system which worked extremely well existed whereby the children were admitted to the Royal Children's Hospital, under the joint care of the Senior Paediatrician of the admitting Unit and the neurologist concerned. Initially, the admitting Unit alternated between the Department of Child Health (Professor Rendle-Short) and Dr R.N. O'Reilly's Medical Unit; later I admitted my patients to the Professorial Unit and Dr Eadie his to Dr O'Reilly's. Because of this system of joint care no figures for neurology in-patients are available. 'Old men forget' and I cannot recall why Dr Felix Arden's Unit was not involved in this system. Throughout the tenure of my appointment at the Royal Children's, Felix and I were good friends and colleagues and when I retired he sent me a charming letter, the contents of which mean a great deal to me. All special neurological procedures and investigations were carried out at the Department of Neurology and Neurosurgery at Royal Brisbane Hospital, the child then being returned to the Royal Children's Hospital.

Admissions to Neurology and Neurosurgery beds at the Royal Brisbane Hospital during the period 1962–66 are listed in Table 3. (*See Appendices*). Over 4,500 patients were admitted, some 1500 being neurological and 3,000 neurosurgical. The latter figure relates only to patients who underwent major surgery. Of the neurological patients, cerebrovascular disease (excluding subarachnoid haemorrhage) was the most frequently encountered disorder, exceeded only by 'epilepsy', if patients with overt cerebral trauma or brain tumour suffering from seizures are included under that heading.

Interunit consultations formed a considerable part of our clinical work. The two neurosurgeons averaged 300–400 consultations each year, excluding head injury cases, while the neurologists undertook 1,445 consultations in other units during the five year period, excluding consultation at the Royal Children's Hospital, Chermside (now Prince Charles) Hospital and consultations with our neurosurgical colleagues.

Neurological investigation has, of course, been revolutionised by computerised tomography (CT scanning) which provides a non-invasive, safe and highly informative diagnostic technique. Since the advent of CT scanning, indications for angiography have been greatly reduced and air encephalography has been rendered almost obsolete. It may be, therefore, of some interest to those brought up in the present era of scanning to look back for a moment to the 1960s.

Carotid angiography dates back to Egaz Moniz of Portugal, who in the late 1920s and early 1930s introduced contrast media, initially sodium iodide and later thorotrast, into the carotid artery which was first exposed by surgical dissection. Partly because of the unsatisfactory nature of the contrast media and partly because open operation was involved, angiography remained in limbo until 1947, when the technique of percutaneous angiography was popularised by Lindgren, while newer contrast media rendered the investigation safer.

Air studies go further back, to the end of the First World War, when the American Walter Dandy in 1918 demonstrated that the ventricular system could be visualised by air introduced directly into the lateral ventricle via a burr hole and cannula and a year later showed that, following lumbar puncture and the withdrawal of cerebrospinal fluid, air injected into the subarachnoid space would enable the ventricular system to be displayed on X-ray film. From 1941 to 1975, the work of the Australian neurologist Graeme Robertson refined fractional air encephalography into something approaching an art form.

Table 4A shows the number of angiograms and air studies performed in the Department during the years 1965 and 1966. We were particularly interested in the issue of normality or abnormality of findings and, in 1967, carried out an audit by studying the records of 358 consecutive new in-patients admitted to the Neurology Unit in 1965–66 to assess the results of the investigations which had been performed (Table 4B). (*See Appendices*)

Unilateral or bilateral carotid angiograms were performed on 125 patients and furnished abnormal results in 15%–20% of cases while air encephalography, carried out on 99 patients, disclosed abnormal findings in 37 instances (37.7%). Of 8 ventriculograms performed, abnormal findings were present in seven patients (87.5%), this high yield of abnormality being due, of course, to the indications for this procedure.

In an article in the *Medical Journal of Australia* reporting the outcome of the ancillary investigations employed at that time (1956–66) in neurological diagnosis my colleagues and I emphasized that the pattern of neurological investigation is evolving continuously and that once a new technique has been fully evaluated and accepted the safest, quickest and most economical way of investigating a particular clinical situation should be employed.

The sole disadvantage of CT scanning would appear to be the cost factor. The very safety of scanning has led to its widespread use as a means of *excluding* a disease process, whereas, because of the discomfort and possible hazard of air studies and angiography the *raison d'etre* for ordering these procedures was to *diagnose* a suspected condition. However, the cost of a CT scan must be evaluated in the context of the cost of hospitalisation, since the vast majority of patients subjected to air studies or angiography were admitted to hospital for these investigations, while such admission is unnecessary for CT scanning.

A further factor to be considered is the growing awareness in the profession that the individual who enters the consulting room, whether it be in hospital or private practice, must be regarded not only as a patient but as a potential litigant. One can hear the voice of a barrister .

> *But I put it to you, doctor, that headache may be a symptom of a brain tumour?*
>
> *Yes.*
>
> *And is it not the case, doctor, that the majority of brain tumours can be diagnosed by a CT brain scan?*

If a comprehensive history and clinical examination dictates the relevance of having a scan performed it should be done in order —

> *... to institute as early as possible all measures which may be indicated for the cure, alleviation and prevention of complications of a patient's illness, and for the protection of others.* [Lord Cohen, 1960]

In this context, ensuring the absence of certain intracranial diseases by a normal scan may have an important bearing on the management of the patient. While CT scanning can not be justified as a routine screening procedure, it is justified if clinical consideration suggests the possibility of structural intracranial change.

Teaching

From 1960 the teaching commitments of the Neurology Unit greatly increased so that, in 1968, Dr Eadie and I shared Professor Tyrer's neurology lectures to fourth year medical students during the Professor's absence on sabbatical leave. a weekly seminar was given to sixth year students on paediatric neurology within the Department of Child Health; there was a weekly teaching round for postgraduates studying for the Diploma of Psychological Medicine (DPM) at the Royal Brisbane Hospital, together with a weekly neurological tutorial for MRACP and DPM candidates, a series of lectures to Speech Therapy students and, finally, the 'Thursday afternoon Neurology Seminars' for fifth and sixth year students and others interested – in addition to postgraduate lecture engagements outwith Brisbane from time to time.

In retrospect, I think the most significant educational activity was the Thursday afternoon seminars. They were tremendous fun and with the blessing of the Department of Medicine and the use of the Sir Edwin Tooth Lecture Theatre they were held from 4.15–5.00 p.m. each Thursday during term, each one being conducted by a member of the Department of Neurology and Neurosurgery.

My good friend Professor Henry Miller wrote in 1968 –

> *The delusion dies hard, especially among Scotsmen and other gloomy academics, that any attempt to make teaching enjoyable is not only sinful but also doomed to failure.*

I think it is safe to say that the Thursday afternoon meetings were both informal and enjoyable. In a Foreword to 'Neurology Seminars of the Royal Brisbane Hospital' (second edition, revised by my two colleagues Dr V.E. Edwards and Dr J.M. Bradfield under the title 'Sutherland's Neurology Seminars of the Royal Brisbane Hospital' – 'revised' mind you, impudent fellows!) and, on this occasion financed by Reckitt and Colman and Roche Products as well as by Smith Kline and French, I wrote 'Neurology and life can be fun and there is room for some light hearted moments and gaiety in the conduct of our profession'.

This was particularly the case when, as happened from time to time, a neurosurgeon and a neurologist would appear together to demonstrate a patient suffering from some disorder of both neurological and neurosurgical interest. After one such occasion in which Ken Jamieson and I had appeared a general practitioner, whose son was a final year student, phoned to say how sorry he was to learn from his son that Ken and I had 'fallen out'. No doubt Ken had swept my tendon hammer on to the floor with a comment such as 'forget the reflexes! Look at the patient; ask yourself – and Sister, has he deteriorated?' And I *may* have rebuked him with a mild 'Angels and Ministers of Grace defend us from neurosurgeons!'

Typed summaries of the condition being demonstrated were prepared and handed out prior to most meetings to allow students to participate in the case demonstration (and appreciate our shafts of wit!) rather than sit with their minds in neutral, taking notes. These summaries were eventually published, in 1975, with the financial assistance of Smith Kline and French, as 'The Neurology Seminars of the Royal Brisbane Hospital'.

The idea of holding Neurology Seminars probably stems from reading the accounts of Byron Bramwell's Clinics at the Royal Infirmary, Edinburgh. The Royal Brisbane Hospital Seminars also proved popular and I can recall the thrill on several occasions of a 'full house', with students sitting on the steps of the aisles. However the seminars had some critics and in 1967, and again in 1968, there were complaints from two other Brisbane Teaching Hospitals that student attendance at these informal, voluntary seminars was having a disruptive influence on their formal teaching programmes. With the support of colleagues in the Department and of the visiting staff of the Hospital the seminars continued on the grounds that it was a service given by the Royal Brisbane Hospital to medical undergraduates and others interested, and since attendance was entirely voluntary the Department of Neurology and Neurosurgery could hardly dictate who could, and who could not, attend.

The Thursday afternoon meetings also proved a forum for distinguished guests and lecturers from interstate and overseas. Unfortunately, I did not keep a 'Visitors Book', but I recall lectures being given by Mr Reginald Hooper (neurosurgeon, Melbourne), and from neurologists J.W. Lance (Sydney), Dr J. Barrie Morley (Melbourne), Sir Kenneth Noad (Sydney), Dr E. Graeme Robertson (Melbourne), and Dr George Selby (Sydney). From overseas we welcomed Professor F.J. Gillingham (neurosurgeon, Royal Infirmary, Edinburgh), and Dr L.T. Kurland (epidemiologist, then of the National Institute of Neurological Disease and Blindness, Bethesda, U.S.A., later of the Mayo Clinic) and, from the United Kingdom, neurologists Dr R.S. Allison (Royal Victoria Hospital, Belfast), Dr William Gooddy (National Hospital for Nervous Diseases and University College Hospital, London). Dr Michael Kremer Middlesex Hospital and National Hospital for Nervous Diseases, London), Dr Harold Millar (Royal Victoria Hospital, Belfast), Professor Henry Miller and Professor Sir John Walton (Royal Victoria Infirmary, Newcastle upon Tyne), and alphabetically last but by no means least, Dr C.W.M. Whitty (Radcliffe Infirmary, Oxford).

We learned from them all and enjoyed their company. I am personally grateful for their advice and for the encouragement and support they gave our Department. I feel, therefore, it is rather invidious to relate anecdotes concerning only a few of our friends but perhaps I will be excused for recalling an occasion in which Professor Eadie with great authority directed traffic around Dr E. Graeme Robertson as, quite unperturbed, the latter set up the tripod of his camera in the middle of a busy thoroughfare in the centre of Brisbane and took photographs of wrought-iron railings which adorned the front of a row of houses. The drama was heightened by the fact that the houses were earmarked for demolition and the irate householders were strongly of the opinion that the photography was a prelude to the loss of their homes.

Len Kurland's visit was my introduction to the American way of life and 'before breakfast' conferences. Len arrived on a late 'plane from Papua-New Guinea and, somewhat tired and also discomfited by forfeiting to Customs spears he had acquired on his travels, retired to bed early but not before expressing a wish for a conference about 4 a.m. next morning. I duly awoke my guest at the appointed hour and for the first (and last) time I sat drinking coffee and discussing multiple sclerosis as the sun rose slowly over Brisbane.

And who could forget William Gooddy's lecture on 'Admiral Lord Nelson's neurological illnesses'. Listening to his paper, members of the audience were translated to the orlop deck of the *Victory* and were present on 21st October, 1815, emotionally moved yet stirred as, in his dying moments, the great Admiral whispered repeatedly 'Thank God, I have done my duty'. This paper was subsequently published in Volume 6 of the *Proceedings of the Australian Association of Neurologists* (1969).

We were also fortunate in having the erudite and entertaining Dr Henry Miller appointed Edwin Tooth Visiting Professor, in 1962.

Professor Henry Miller
Consultant Neurologist and Dean of the
Faculty of Medicine, Newcastle-upon-Tyne.

Already something of a legend in neurological circles, as I was to write in the book *Remembering Henry*, 'His visit to Brisbane was a signal success. Henry was no cold, sterile academician. He imparted knowledge and wisdom with consummate oratory, both at teaching rounds and at formal lectures'. In the course of one teaching round we were discussing the nature of a sixth cranial nerve palsy which had afflicted a middle aged lady from North Queensland. Despite angiography and other investigations the aetiology had eluded us. 'You know, John,' Henry commented,

MAP 8: ' ... *it is over 700 miles by air from Townsville to Brisbane* ...'

'you *do* over investigate your patients'. I swallowed. 'Is that so? You must remember it is over 700 miles by air from Townsville where the lady lives to Brisbane – rather more than between Carlisle and Newcastle', I retorted somewhat smugly. 'No excuse! The aetiology of idiopathic sixth nerve palsy is equally idiopathic in Townsville as it is in Carlisle!'

We flavoured many other 'Millerisms' such as the play on words in –

Headache which wakens the patient from sleep is always organic, even if it is only alcohol.

and the advice that –

Fainting at prayers is another reason for removing religion from the school curriculum.

One weekend was spent cruising in Moreton Bay on a cabin cruiser owned by Dr David Henderson, a senior physician at The Royal Brisbane Hospital, and his brother Bob, a well known Queensland stockbroker. In addition to the Hendersons, Henry and myself, the 'crew' also included a legal luminary and Dr Donald Watson, a senior orthopaedic surgeon. The stage was set for an entertaining weekend and after dropping anchor on the Friday evening the Ship's Company dined and wined well, the tide of conversation carrying us into the early hours of Saturday morning.

Unfortunately, I was wakened from sleep by an attack of migraine which occasioned the only diagnostic blunder of Henry's visit. Hearing the moans of anguish emanating from my bunk Henry glared balefully at me 'Sutherland, you have a hangover' and, in an airy aside to the others, 'Let's have a nice dry riesling with our scrambled eggs', a remark which did nothing to ease my suffering.

Professor Henry Miller, on the high seas in the care of JMS.
Moreton Bay, 1963.

However, 'touch not the cat ... ' as the Sutherland motto has it and I tasted the sweetness of revenge next day. While our companions were preparing lunch — and pre-lunch cocktails — Henry and I enjoyed a swim off the boat. As we were disporting ourselves Henry remarked 'I have just seen a huge fish'. Now in my book all 'huge fish' in Moreton Bay are sharks until proven otherwise and on receipt of Henry's information I made record time to the safety of the boat. From this advantageous position, while towelling myself, I informed Henry conversationally of my views on the probable species of his 'huge fish'. The speed with which Henry George Miller covered the few yards to the boat and the agility with which he hauled himself on board was equalled only by the wealth of abuse to which I was then subjected.

From time to time 'Postgraduate Neurological week-ends' were organised and hosted by the Department with the co-operation of the Postgraduate Medical Education Committee, the University of Queensland, the Queensland Faculty of the Royal Australian College of General Practitioners, and the Royal Brisbane and Royal Children's Hospitals. These weekends differed widely in format. Sometimes, various aspects of a neurological–neurosurgical topic or theme were discussed by a guest lecturer and staff members, as for example, in May, 1972, when 'Parkinsonism and other extrapyramidal disorders' was the topic, or in October, 1974, 'Problems in epilepsy in general practice'. On other occasions, as in June 1965, and July 1969, demonstrations, held concurrently mainly on investigatory techniques, and a film on clinical neurological examination or the detection of Parkinsonism, occupied much of the Saturday morning and was followed by symposia on various topics and, perhaps, a clinico-pathological conference on Saturday afternoon and Sunday morning.

'Teaching by the printed page' was not ignored and the history of books first published from the early days of the Department to the time of my retiral from the visiting staff, is indicated in Table 5. (*See Appendices*) In addition, members of the Department contributed chapters and articles to other publications.

Research

In the early years of the Department of Neurology and Neurosurgery, research was essentially at the clinical and epidemiological levels with a dash of laboratory and histological investigations supplied by Dr M.J. Eadie in regard to Parkinsonism and, later, quantitative microscopic enzyme histochemistry.

Several themes of clinical and epidemiological research were followed in association with Dr Eadie and Professor Tyrer (Table 6). My own particular interest in multiple sclerosis continued (Table 7) (*see Appendices*) and I was honoured by a visit from Professor Helmut J. Bauer, Universitat Gottingen, West Germany, who presented me with an etching and an appreciation of the epidemiological work carried out by my Unit.

Our interest in congenital and degenerative conditions embraced tuberose sclerosis, hemifacial atrophy, muscle dystrophy and, in

Dr John Pearn, Registrar to Dr John Sutherland at the Royal Children's Hospital, Brisbane 1968-1971.
Later, Professor of Child Health, and close friend of the author.

particular, the spino-cerebellar degenerations. Our colleague Dr John Pearn (now Professor Pearn) of the Royal Children's Hospital, had similar interests and during his tenure as the first holder of the Florey Fellowship carried out an impressive series of genetic and clinical studies into the spinal muscular atrophies.

Neuro-ocular disorders included a study of the ocular manifestations in 558 patients with multiple sclerosis, the eleventh report in the literature of carotid-cavernous sinus fistula with contra-lateral signs, a study of benign monocular blindness (*amaurosis fugax*), and a series of unusual abnormalities of internal and external ocular movements. This last was published in *Revue Neurologique,* a fact which drew a comment from Dr Roland P. Mackay, editor of the *Year Book of Neurology, Psychiatry and Neurosurgery* (1964–65 series).

Mervyn Eadie and I shared an interest in migrainous neuralgia (cluster headache) and in 1972 published the results of our studies on fifty-eight patients suffering from this disorder. We were gratified to receive a letter from Professor Ottar Sjaastad of Trondheim University Hospital, Norway, in 1986 in which he generously wrote:

> ... *I have extensively used your article from 1972, which I think still is one of the major sources of information concerning the clinical manifestations of cluster headache ... it emanates from my chapter that I really have relied on your data'.* [In the revised series of *Handbook of Clinical Neurology*].

Fleet-footed the busy years passed, expedited by a considerable amount of travel within Australia and overseas. Over the years 1961-1972, I spent three weeks in Singapore and Penang as a member of an Australian team of doctors invited by the Committee on Postgraduate Medical Studies of the University of Singapore, and the Royal Australasian College of Physicians to lecture on advanced Medicine – in my case neurology, and gave papers at Queen Square, London, the Massachusetts General Hospital, Boston and in Tokyo, Goteborg, Newcastle upon Tyne and Glasgow.

These were years during which I did not see my family sufficiently but we did share the enjoyment of family holidays, usually at Cabarita over the Christmas period and at Yamba in August. The pleasure of these holidays was enhanced by *Blue Wing*, a 16 foot half-cabin cruiser (probably the outcome of genetic prompting by my distant crofter–fishermen ancestors!) which Iain and I had convinced Pat, somewhat to our surprise, was an essential family acquisition. Gillian and Iain and their friends learned to ski in her wake at Cabarita, while at Yamba *Blue Wing* was used daily for fishing and cruising on the Clarence estuary and river.

In common with all boats 'things happen'. I recall *Bracken*, our golden cocker spaniel, disappearing overboard in hot pursuit of pelicans, of boat and trailer (and car!) being stranded on a busy boat-ramp when the slave cylinder of the Jaguar's clutch suddenly gave up the ghost. I remember a case of mutinous behaviour — Iain at the wheel, Gillian at the bow, *Blue Wing* approaching a jetty at a considerable rate of knots.

> **Iain:** *Fend off, for'ard Gill!*
> **Gillian** (turning aft, arms akimbo):
> *Don't you dare shout at me like that!*
> *Fend off yourself!*

On another occasion, Pat and Iain in *Blue Wing* were towing the dinghy with me aboard out to our buoy at Cleveland. As I stood up to adjust something in the bow my feet slipped. I fell forward and the bow of the light aluminium dinghy dipped under the water. With considerable way on and before I could transfer my weight aft, the little vessel filled with water and slowly sank. In true naval fashion I stood saluting before swimming to *Blue Wing.* Pat and Iain, convulsed with laughter, proved of little assistance in hauling me aboard.

During my adult life I have been an unrepentant car buff. In Britain, my pride and joy had been a Triumph Roadster and when my family outgrew that, an Alvis. An Austin 105 accompanied us to Australia and figures in the Hospital photograph along with Ken Jamieson's MG Magnette saloon. After the statutory duty free period had elapsed I became a Jaguar devotee, a Mark 2, 2.4 being followed by a 3.8, an S type and finally an E type. The E type, perhaps because of its general appearance, appeared to arouse concupiscent elements hidden in the character of my friends. Ken Jamieson referred to my E type as 'Sutherland's menopausal syndrome'. Cardiologist J.H.N. Bett went one better by sending me a series of illustrations depicting 'primary sex characteristics, secondary sex characteristics' and 'for those who need it, a tertiary sex characteristic' — a photograph of an E type Jaguar.

'A thing of beauty...'

The E type jaguar, which '...appeared to arouse concupiscent elements hidden in the character of my friends ... '

Photo, 1969.

Cars have brought me a great deal of pleasure and the opportunity of friendships I value such as those with Jim Abercrombie, Bill Pitt, Glyn Scott and Clive Nolan. Jim Abercrombie, one time service manager at Westco when they held the Jaguar franchise in Brisbane, taught me a lot about cars, and Bill Pitt, Australian Touring Car Champion in 1961, about driving. This interest led me to become a medical officer at first to the old Lowood track and later at Lakeside.

While writing of *Blue Wing* I mentioned *Bracken*, our golden cocker spaniel. We have been a 'doggy' family. I was brought up with dogs, mainly collies and gun dogs in Caithness, but even in Glasgow there was generally a Cairn terrier in the house. A liking for dogs was also present on Pat's side of our family because her mother once told her 'Before you marry, be sure your future husband has been good to his mother and fond of dogs.'

Two of our dogs — the pup's fig leaf (left) by courtesy of my friend Mr Bell Fletcher, the photographer.

Unfortunately, I never had a chance to be good to my mother, unless I was a good baby, which my family thinks unlikely, but I have been fond of dogs and, perhaps a bonus point, fond of horses.

In Australia we have owned, in addition to *Bracken*, a rough coat Scottish Collie (*Lisa*), a black and white spaniel (*Wee Geordie*), a German Shepherd (*Heidi*) and our present incumbents, a Border Collie (*Tina*) and a long haired German Shepherd (*Honey*).

There has been no 'best dog' or best breed. They have all been 'good' with different personalities, habits, likes, dislikes, peculiarities and endearing ways. We have enjoyed their companionship, admired their loyalty and have appreciated their presence in our home and in our lives. To fully enjoy dogs one has to 'get into their skin' to understand their psychological make-up, and for those interested in doing this I would commend unreservedly *Man meets dog* by Konrad Lorenz MD (Vienna), PhD (Vienna). Dr Lorenz is a zoologist, psychologist and neuropsychiatrist. He is an animal and in particular a dog lover but unlike some dog-loving neurologists he is an excellent and entertaining writer.

My private practice flourished, initially at Selby House, Wickham Terrace. Selby House was an old building. Our rooms were on the ground floor but in the basement there was a rather good restaurant (*Chez Tessa*), and the most delicious odours would percolate into my consulting room through the elderly floorboards. Ken Jamieson and I, and shortly afterwards Mervyn Eadie, had our rooms on one side of a large central waiting-room—reception area while Howard Tait and the electroencephalography laboratory occupied the other side. In the early 1960s, it was not uncommon for Dr Tait and me to work on a Saturday morning and on such occasions Pat would accompany me, acting as my receptionist–secretary. As part of her 'duties' she would make coffee for the three of us about 11 a.m. On one occasion, when the waiting-room was reasonably full with patients and their relatives, I took a patient I had just seen out to Pat's desk to arrange for X-rays and EEG to be performed during the following week. I turned to go back to my room when Pat so far forgot herself to enquire from me in a carrying voice 'DARLING, would you like a coffee now?' Patients sat bolt upright. Magazines were lowered and eyebrows raised at this evidence of an 'affair' between the doctor and his secretary.

In 1964, we all moved to Ladhope Chambers, Wickham Terrace. Dr Yelland joined Dr Jamieson in one suite, Dr Eadie and I shared an adjoining one with psychiatrists Howard Tait and Bill Hamilton and the electroencephalogram laboratory occupying the remainder of the fourth floor.

In addition to clinical neurology I developed an interest in neurological medico-legal work which has continued to the present time. There has been, of course, a relationship between Medicine and the Law since the dawn of history, when priests combined the roles of lawgiver, judge and physician. As Sir William Osler said –

> *The practice of Medicine is an art based on science,*
> *the art consisting largely of balancing probabilities.*

Similarly, in Law, judgements are made on a preponderance of probabilities. Despite our common ancestry and similarities in training and techniques, many doctors eschew Court work. Aside from the obvious reasons of inconvenience, a non-familiar environment and perhaps a nagging fear of being embarrassed, I think dislike of medico-legal work has its basis in two factors, in two essential differences between Medicine and the Law. As doctors we are trained to arrive hopefully at the truth – the correct diagnosis, whereas lawyers and barristers, in our adversary system of Justice, draw deductions from the evidence to suit their clients' best interests often by ignoring, negating, or challenging facts which do not serve their purpose. By serving but one client – the truth, the medical witness will of necessity be in conflict with one or other side in a Court of Law and tends to resent what he or she regards as an attempt to corrupt the evidence leading to the truth. However, provided the medical witness sticks to facts and does not stray outside his field of knowledge or expertise, he can be confident that in the majority of cases the judge will deduce from the evidence he has heard where the truth indeed lies.

Again to quote Osler,

> *Law constantly looking back, has its forms and procedures, its precedents and practices,* [whereas Medicine] *... has a progressive character ... with the sole exception of the mechanical sciences, no other department of human knowledge has undergone so profound a change ... .*

This lack of change in civil legal processes, the delays and the uncertainties as to whether one will be required on a certain day to give evidence, combine to make the medical man wary of undertaking voluntarily medico-legal work.

Margaret and 'Snow' Ash were our good friends and next door neighbours in Indooroopilly. We held them both in very affectionate regard and were deeply grieved by Margaret's death while still a young woman. This crystallised our thoughts that one day we would move to the Moreton Bay area.

In due course we discovered an ideal site at Cleveland overlooking Moreton Bay, Peel Island and, in the distance, North Stradbroke Island. There we had a house built on a site occupied many years earlier by the home of a doctor, added a boat house and later a private ramp. We changed our address from Harts Road, Indooroopilly to Shore Street, Cleveland in 1971.

I have written much about myself but little of my family, Pat, Gillian and Iain.

Since our marriage in 1944, Pat has been a tremendous support to me. She is intensely loyal to everyone and everything she holds dear. Undoubtedly, if I have accomplished anything it is largely due to Pat's backing, interest, compassion and care of us as a family. As I indicated in the dedication of my book *Fundamentals of Neurology*, I have been helped in my life and career by many people —

> ... *my wife, my colleagues, the registrars, house officers, students, nursing and paramedical staff of the Department of Neurology and Neurosurgery, the Royal Brisbane Hospital* ... .

I have no hesitation in describing Pat as being the keystone of my happy family life and of my professional career.

Wherever we have lived Pat has transformed a 'house' into a 'home'. This ability is an inherent characteristic and does not depend on wealth or beautiful furnishings, a quality which Gillian has also inherited. When our friend, accountant and 'business manager', Mr David Tanner was less than impressed with *Glentor*, our proposed new house and our present home, his business associate Karen (now Mrs Spicer), supported us with the comment 'Wait, David, until Pat has made it a home', and that is exactly what she has done.

I have no prescription for a happy married life other than to recommend a mix of affection, loyalty, respect, forbearance, humour and common interests. Pat has these qualities and I have been fortunate in sharing forty-four years of married life with her.

Our two children, Gillian and Iain, both went to school in Australia, initially at Ironsides State School, Indooroopilly, Gillian then being ten and Iain five years of age. Iain had at this time a very broad Scottish accent and because of this was teased by his peers at school. For a month or so he became virtually aphasic but must have been practising when alone in his room because Pat and I were visibly shaken when one day he came out with 'Where's moi boike?' in the broadest of Australian accents.

The marriage of Gillian Sutherland and Donald McKee.
Gillian arriving at the Church with JMS.
January 10th, 1970,

THE McKEE FAMILY

Left to Right: Louise, Jennifer, Gillian (née Sutherland) and Donald McKee.
Photograph, May 1988.

Gillian later attended Brisbane Girls Grammar School, becoming a Prefect in her last year. Iain attended Brisbane Boys College. Both did well scholastically despite spending five months in Scotland in 1961, where they did a correspondence course aided by a tutor in Stirling. By this time Iain had acquired a normal Australian accent which, however, did not go well with Robert Burns' 'Wee sleekit cowrin, tim'rous beastie' address *To a Mouse* which his Scottish tutor insisted he should learn.

After obtaining a good Senior examination pass Gillian proceeded to Queensland University, where she read for her BA and then attended Kelvin Grove Teachers Training College, where she took her Diploma in Education. While she was teaching at St Hilda's Boarding School, Southport, she and Donald McKee became engaged to be married. Don had already graduated BSc and had achieved his Master's degree in Metallurgy and was working towards his PhD when they were married in January, 1970. With two daughters, Jennifer born on 3rd May, 1972, and Louise on 4th June, 1974, they now live in Brisbane where Don is a senior member of staff of the Mining Department of Queensland University.

Iain enjoyed life at Brisbane Boys College, eventually in his final year becoming a Prefect, a sergeant in the Training Corps Band, and playing rugby for the 'social' third XV and sometimes to his horror for the second XV, who took life and especially rugby much more seriously. On leaving school Iain became a medical student, largely because at that time he could not think of anything else to do. He was, however, not cut out for the life of a medical student and left University in first year Medicine. He was accepted by the Australian Army as an Officer Cadet and in the army found his niche. He was physically fit for the arduous training course and mentally bright so that the required study and examinations presented no difficulty. He enjoyed army life and the fellowship of like-minded lads. A reasonably experienced free-fall parachutist, he was engaged in this hobby in the hope of improving his chances of eventually joining the Parachute Regiment when on 26th August, 1973, on his second jump, his parachute and the reserve 'chute' failed to open ...

PREFECTS AND SUB-PREFECTS, BRISBANE BOYS COLLEGE, 1969.
Iain Sutherland, middle row, far right.

PIPE BAND OF THE BRISBANE BOYS COLLEGE
Iain Sutherland, front row, far left. Photo, 1969.

193

Probably I was becoming 'burned out' anyway, but certainly after Iain's death I lost a great deal of drive and enthusiasm. By this time, the Neurology Unit was fully staffed. At the Children's Hospital, Dr John Pearn was Reader in Child Health and Dr Barry Appleton had returned from St Louis where he had received specialised training in paediatric neurology, and from Glasgow where he had gained further experience with Professor John Simpson at the Institute of Neurological Sciences, Southern General Hospital.

Table 8 (*see Appendix*) indicates the staff of the Department of Neurology and Neurosurgery, including the Royal Children's Hospital, when I resigned my hospital appointments in June, 1975. I was very honoured to be appointed Honorary Consultant Neurologist to the Royal Brisbane and Royal Children's Hospitals and I was not cut off from my old colleagues as I continued my private practice at Ladhope. Six months later, on 25th January, 1976, John Yelland 'phoned me the news of Ken Jamieson's sudden death. It had become increasingly difficult for Pat and me to continue living in a house which held so many memories of a happier past and with the McKee family in Colorado for a few years and with Ken's death, preceded by Howard Tait's, the catalysts for further action were to hand. After much thought and discussion, and with the professional wisdom and advice of our friend and accountant Mr David Tanner, we elected to move to Toowoomba and left *Seacroft* and Ladhope Chambers in 1977.

A FAR OFF SUNLIT PLACE

TOOWOOMBA

s I sit writing this in my study at *Glentor*, I am surrounded by unspoiled country – fields, cattle, farms, trees and hills, and a great quiet. *Glentor* is situated in the Shire of Cambooya, south-west of Toowoomba but as they say in the advertisement 'only 15 minutes from the centre of the city'. The Shire is triangular in shape with its apex to the north and the City of Toowoomba. its eastern border is the Great Dividing Range, its western the rolling Darling Downs, and its base to the south, centred on the township of Clifton.

Scots have a terrible pride of country, of belonging to Scotland, and this is particularly true whether they be separated from their homeland by choice or by circumstances, as witness the nostalgic nature of many traditional Scottish songs.

> *Far off in sunlit places, sad are the Scottish faces,*
> *Yearning to feel the kiss of sweet Scottish rain,*
> *Where tropic skies are beaming, love sets the heart*
> *   adreaming,*
> *Longing and dreaming for the homeland again.*

(Scotland the Brave)

195

Although the climate is quite different, superficially the landscape surrounding *Glentor* is not unlike that of Scotland. Certainly bushland replaces heather, bracken and whin, the trees are eucalypts instead of pines, and the hills are not so high and craggy as the Grampians, but as in the Highlands of Scotland —

Where essential silence cheers and blesses
And for ever in the hill-recesses
Her more lovely music
Broods and dies.

(*In the Highlands:* Robert Louis Stevenson)

Pat and I have found tranquility at *Glentor.*

After coming to Toowoomba in 1977, I continued to practice clinical neurology to the end of 1985. As there was no neurologist attending Toowoomba General Hospital, I offered to undertake an out-patient session and EEG reporting. Dr D.A. O'Rourke, the medical superintendent, accepted this offer and I continued to be visiting neurologist to the Hospital until 1981. On relinquishing my appointment to a younger visiting neurologist I was honoured by Dr O'Rourke and the Hospital Board who appointed me Honorary Consultant Neurologist to the Hospital.

In 1978, with only a part-time recordist at Toowoomba General Hospital, EEGs were performed on only two days per week and totalled 340 tracings in that year, an average of some 30 per month. With the development of the Department, including a staff of one trained recordist and one trainee, the number of recordings carried out more than doubled, 70–75 being performed each month suggesting that when a service is readily available it will be utilised for the benefit of patients.

During this time, and prior to 1980, I also learned that young neurologists prefer the challenge of the larger centres to a country town and district. In the late 1970s Dr O'Rourke and I arranged for a notice to appear in a circular of the Australian Association of Neurologists indicating the availability of hospital neurological sessions in Toowoomba and the possibility of being associated with a private neurological practice with, however, there being no enquiries.

I also visited the Baillie Henderson Psychiatric Hospital in a consulting and teaching capacity and as there was no neurologist resident in Toowoomba, and no visiting neurologist, I undertook a limited amount of private practice from the rooms of my good friends Dr John Howell, initially, and later Drs Fabian and Jean Bryant.

St Vincent's Hospital, Toowoomba, is an acute private hospital of some 200 beds with medical, surgical, paediatric and obstetric wards and radiological (including ultrasound and CT scanning)

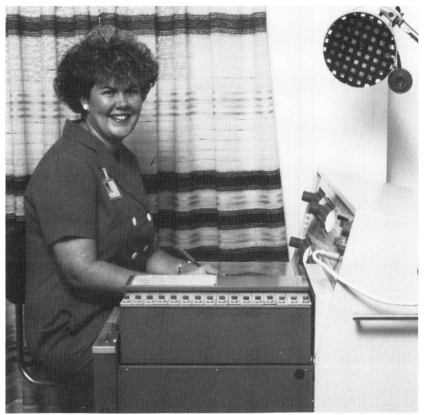

Mrs A Pyke, Senior Secretary to the Neurology Unit at St Vincent's Hospital, Toowoomba, and EEG Recordist. Photo, 1988, by courtesy of Mr David Seeto.

Mrs Mullins, EEG Recordist, St Vincent's Hospital, Toowoomba.
Photo, 1988, by courtesy of Mr David Seeto.

and pathology services. In 1980, Sister Anthea Groves RSC, the
Sister Administrator of St Vincent's Hospital, was given permission
by the Superior General and Council of The Sisters of Charity, and
by the State Health Department, to rent me accommodation in the
Hospital for the purposes of setting up an EEG Department and in
1981 a suite of rooms was also made available for clinical use.

Dr N.S. Saines FRACP, Consultant Neurologist.
Photographed at St Vincent's Hospital, Toowoomba, 1988,
by Mr David Seeto.

Closing of the Sutherland Seminar on Contemporary Neurology and Neurosurgery, 30th August 1986, at Toowoomba. Left to Right . Dr John Bradfield, Dr John Sutberland, and Dr John Lockwood MLA.

Setting up an EEG laboratory in a private hospital was not a new venture as for many years my colleagues and I had serviced an EEG Unit we established at St Andrew's Hospital, Brisbane. St Andrew's Hospital, Brisbane and St Vincent's Hospital, Toowoomba, are the two private hospitals I have been most closely associated with and my admiration for the two senior administrators of these hospitals, Miss Annat ('Pixie') in Brisbane and Sister Anthea in Toowoomba (now at St Vincent's Hospital, Melbourne), is boundless. The need for the St Vincent's EEG Department is apparent from the increase in the number of records performed, 242 from April to December, 1980, and 559 in 1981, to over 1,000 in each of the last three years (1985, 1986, 1987). The majority of tracings are performed on a 16 channel Siemens Elema, an 8 channel Nihon Kohden being well used as necessary (for example, in theatre to monitor carotid artery surgery), with an 8 channel Neuroscribe SLE in reserve.

Dr N.S. Saines, visiting neurologist to the Mater Misericordiae Hospital, Brisbane, became associated with me at St Vincent's some five years ago and combines most effectively the skills of a clinician with those of a highly trained neurophysiologist. As a result, electromyography, nerve conduction studies and evoked potentials are now available at St Vincent's Hospital, together with a non-invasive vascular investigation facility.

At the end of 1985, I retired completely from clinical practice but continued medico-legal work and electroencephalography. Dr Saines now consults at Toowoomba on three days each week, supplying a very adequate clinical service.

In August, 1986, a Symposium 'Contemporary Neurology and Neurosurgery' was held at Toowoomba in my honour, a continuation of the annual seminars held by the Department of Neurology and Neurosurgery each winter, but for the first time held outside Brisbane. This was made possible by the generous help of Sandoz Pharmaceuticals, a drug firm I have had friendly association with over many years. I was particularly pleased Dr Mulhearn of Sandoz and Mr Carl P. Meade, their Queensland Manager, both old friends, could be present and greatly honoured that Dr George Selby, accompanied by Mrs Selby, made the long trip from Sydney to Toowoomba to be the Guest Speaker. As twenty-five of my old friends and colleagues sat down to dinner that evening in Lords Restaurant to honour Pat and me I felt both humble and proud that they should hold me in such regard.

Life in Toowoomba has been a most pleasant form of semi-retirement. I was invited to write a short textbook of neurology based on the 'Seminars of the Royal Brisbane Hospital'. Although not highly successful when published as *Fundamentals of Neurology* (Adis, 1981), it was rather good fun to write and helped to crystallise some of my own thoughts on various neurological topics.

In 1985 the Department of Child Health, University of Queensland, unveiled the memorial John MacKay Sutherland Barometer, in the Lecture Theatre, Royal Children's Hospital, Brisbane. Left to Right . Professor Mervyn Eadie, Dr John Sutherland, and Dr Vivian Edwards.

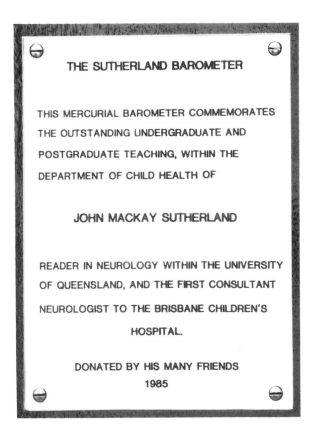

THE SUTHERLAND BAROMETER

THIS MERCURIAL BAROMETER COMMEMORATES
THE OUTSTANDING UNDERGRADUATE AND
POSTGRADUATE TEACHING, WITHIN THE
DEPARTMENT OF CHILD HEALTH OF

JOHN MACKAY SUTHERLAND

READER IN NEUROLOGY WITHIN THE UNIVERSITY
OF QUEENSLAND, AND THE FIRST CONSULTANT
NEUROLOGIST TO THE BRISBANE CHILDREN'S
HOSPITAL.

DONATED BY HIS MANY FRIENDS
1985

203

'A SUNLIT PLACE'

*Grand-daughters Louise (left) and Jennifer McKee, with their namesakes.
Photo, 1985.*

For some years Pat and I enjoyed playing golf at Middle Ridge but, unfortunately, increasing arthritic changes in my knees, the outcome of too many years, too much football and too many miles of hill walking has prevented us continuing a game we both greatly enjoyed. I am still able to exercise my dogs on our twelve acres of bushland, look after two donkeys (named *Jenny* and *Louise* after my grandchildren!) and keep my fifteen year old Mercedes Coupe in immaculate condition — and read books I have never had time to read in the past. The McKee family pays us regular visits as does my good friend Mervyn Eadie, and we appreciate and look forward to their visits.

Professor Eadie was very complimentary about me in the booklet of the proceedings of the Symposium held in my honour in 1986, and I was highly honoured that the Australian Association of Neurologists saw fit to make me an Honorary Member Emeritus of the Association, indeed a signal honour from one's colleagues and one I deeply appreciate. The fact of the matter is, however, that I was simply in the right place at the right time and had colleagues whose loyalty was complete and whose abilities, expertise and originality were always available to me. Osler was, indeed, correct in saying —

*Through your students and your disciples will come
your greatest honour.*

'LIFE IN THE BUSH'

Our Shetland pony 'Whisky',
bred by Dr and Mrs Vivian Edwards,
with JMS. Photo, 1980

And that is my story ... with the benefit of hindsight all doubts and errors are removed and looking back over the span of years it is natural to reflect on the various Rubicons that were encountered. Should I have remained in Inverness, or in Britain? Should I have continued on the whole-time staff of the University of Queensland? Should I have done this – or that?

For my part I have no regrets. Although I look out of my study on 'green hills that are not Highland hills', Australia has been good to me. I have had the benefit of a happy married life and have thoroughly enjoyed the combination of University–Hospital and private practice I was able to follow for many years. In particular, Toowoomba has been kind in allowing me to achieve a graduated retiral from active practice in pleasant surroundings.

One has to tread the path one sees; it may even lead to 'far off sunlit places'.

APPENDICES

TABLE 1

Department of Neurology and Neurosurgery — 1967

CONSULTANT STAFF

NEUROLOGISTS

Senior Visiting Neurologist	— JM Sutherland, MD, FRCP(Ed), FRACP
Junior Visiting Neurologist	— MJ Eadie, MD, MRACP
Assistant Visiting Neurologist	— MEB Murphy, MB, BS, MRACP

NEUROSURGEONS

Senior Bisiting Neurosurgeon	— KG Jamieson, MS, FRACS
Junior Visiting Neurosurgeon	— JDN Yelland, FRCS, FRACS

ANAESTHETISTS

Visiting Anaesthetist	— T O'Rourke Brophy, FFARCS, FFARACS, DA
Visiting Anaesthetist	— PD Livingstone, MB BS, DA (Melb)
Staff Anaesthetists	— D Jackson, FFARCS, FFARACS
	— G Hickson, BA, MB BS, DA

NEURORADIOLOGIST	— PA Tod, FCRA
NEUROPATHOLOGIST	— M Mead, MCPA
RADIOTHERAPIST	— KW Mead, DMRT, FCRA, FFR

TABLE 1 (contd)

ELECTROENCEPHALOGRAPHERS— WH Tait, DPM, RCP & S
    — MJ Eadie, MD, MRACP
    — JE Edwards, MRACP, DPM
    — MEB Murphy, MRACP

NEUROPTHALMOLOGIST   — H Fraser, MB, BS, DO, RCP & S

RESIDENT STAFF

NEUROLOGY REGISTRAR   — P Mann, MRACP

NEUROSURGERY REGISTRAR   — P Miller, FRACS

RADIOLOGY REGISTRAR   — W Gale   J Earwacker
  (in rotation)   D Jones   M Uhr

REGISTRARS IN ANAESTHESIA — D McConnell   J Haines
                              W Power   A Baker

RESIDENT MEDICAL OFFICERS

    Neurology   — Drs Behan, Paterson, Meares,
                              Bowden and Buttwell

    Neurosurgery   — Drs McMahon, Taylor, Williams

NURSING STAFF

Senior Ward Sister   — Sister M Lochrin

Sister in Charge, Operating Theatre — Sister P Kinghorn

Appendices

TABLE 2

**Attendances at Royal Brisbane Hospital,
Neurology–Neurosurgical Unit
Out-patients Department – 1962–66**

OUT–PATIENT ATTENDANCE

	NEUROLOGY	NEUROSURGERY	
Year	New Cases	New Cases	Follow-Up/Review
1962	368	82	807
1963	409	63	809
1964	487	86	821
1965	379	85	705
1966	283	79	543
Totals	1,926	395	3,685

TABLE 3

**Admissions to Neurology–Neurosurgical Department
1962–66**

ADMISSIONS

YEAR	NEUROLOGY			NEUROSURGERY*
	New Patients	Readmissions	Total	
1962	332	28	360	545
1963	316	16	332	569
1964	282	37	319	594
1965	229	38	267	581
1966	328	10	338	689
Totals	1,487	129	1,616	2,978

*These figures relate only to patients undergoing major surgical procedures:
patients admitted only for investigation and/or non-surgical care
are not included.

Appendices

TABLE 4A

DIAGNOSTIC NEURORADIOLOGY
1965–66
ANGIOGRAPHY

YEAR	CAROTID		VERTEBRAL		TOTAL
	Unilateral	Bilateral	Unilateral	Bilateral	
1965	549	726	44	46	1365
1966	532	628	47	8	1215

AIR STUDIES

	Pneumoencephalograms		Ventriculograms	Total
	Adult	Under 12 Years		
1965	368	97	132	597
1966	275	39	116	430

TABLE 4B

Investigations performed in 358 Neurological In-patients

(After Sutherland, Eadie, Mann & Tyrer, 1967)

INVESTIGATIONS	NO. OF PATIENTS		ABNORMAL RESULT	
	No.	%	No.	%
X-ray chest	264	73.7	25	9.5
X-ray skull	242	67.6	16	6.6
Electroencephalography	242	67.6	133	54.9
Lumbar puncture elective	33	9.2		
CSF obtained during other	160	44.8	35	21.9
Investigations	127	35.6		
Air encephalography	99	27.7	37	37.3
Ventriculography	8	2.2	7	87.5
Angiography	125	34.9	24	19.2

Appendices

TABLE 5

Books first published during 1962–1975 by members of the Department of Neurology and Neurosurgery

Sutherland JM

Your child and epilepsy. Brisbane, Queensland Health Education Council for Brisbane Children's Hospital. 1963.

Jamieson KG

A first notebook of head injury. Brisbane. Jacaranda Press. 1965.

Jamieson KG, Tait H

Traffic injury in Brisbane. Canberra. NHMRC. 1966.

Tyrer JH, Sutherland JM

Exercises in neurological diagnosis. Edinburgh. Livingstone. 1967.

Sutherland JM, Tait H

The epilepsies: modern diagnosis and treatment. Edinburgh. Livingstone. 1969.

Jamieson KG

A first notebook of head injury. 2nd ed. London. Butterworths. 1971.

Sutherland JM, Tait H, Eadie MJ

The epilepsies: modern diagnosis and treatment. 2nd ed. Edinburgh. Churchill-Livingstone. 1974.

Sutherland JM ed.

Symposium on epilepsy, Brisbane, October, 1974 Sydney. Madden House for Parke-Davis.

Bain C, Jamieson KG, Robertson JS

A national survey of Ambulance Service operations. 1975.

Tyrer JH, Sutherland JM

Exercises in neurological diagnosis. 2nd ed. Edinburgh. Churchill-Livingstone. 1975.

Tyrer JH, Sutherland JM

Esercitazioni pratiche di neuroligia. Roma: *Il Pensiero Scientifico.* 1975.

Sutherland JM, ed.

Neurology seminars of the Royal Brisbane Hospital. Published on behalf of Smith Kline and French, 1975.

Appendices

TABLE 5 (contd)

Sutherland JM, Tait H, Eadie MJ	Epilepsias: diagnostico y tratamiento. Mexico. *El Manual Moderno.* 1977
Edwards VE, Bradfield JM	eds. *Sutherland's Neurology Seminars of the Royal Brisbane Hospital.* Brisbane. Published on behalf of Reckitt and Colman, Roche Products, Smith Kline and French, 1979.
Sutherland JM, Eadie MJ	*The epilepsies; modern diagnosis and treatment.* 3rd ed. Edinburgh. Churchill Livingstone. 1980.
Tyrer JH, Sutherland JM Eadie MJ	*Exercises in neurological diagnosis.* 3rd ed. Edinburgh: Churchill Livingstone, 1981.
Sutherland JM, Tait H, Eadie MJ	Epilepsias, diagnostico y tratamiento. 2nd ed. Mexico: *El Manual Moderno,* 1982.
Sutherland JM, Eadie MJ	*La Epilessie; diagnosi e cura attuali.* Palermo: Medical Books di G. Cafaro. 1984.

TABLE 6

RESEARCH TOPICS 1962–75

SUBJECT OF RESEARCH	NUMBER OF PAPERS
Multiple sclerosis	9
Congenital and degenerative disorders	7
Epilepsy	6
Neuroocular abnormalities	6
Headache and migraine	5
Parkinson's disease	4
Cryptococcosis of the central nervous system	2
Miscellaneous subjects	6

Appendices

TABLE 7

RESULTS OF INVESTIGATIONS INTO MULTIPLE SCLEROSIS

1. Clinical and serological features of MS patients in Queensland similar to those reported elsewhere.

2. The disease affects both Australian born white population and recent migrants in almost equal numbers.

3. The disease is extremely rare in Australian aborigines, New Zealand maoris, native Fijians and in the Indian population of Fiji.

4. Prevalence rate for Queensland (10–29 S latitude) is 13–15/100,000

5. The disease is more common in latitudes greater than $35°S$.
    e.g. Perth, WA $(31°57°)$
    Newcastle, NSW $(32°52°)$ } 20/100,000

    Hobart, Tasmania $(42°50°)$ 32/100,000

(from –
    Sutherland, Tyrer and Eadie, 1961:
    Sutherland, Tyrer and Eadie, 1962:
    Eadie and Sutherland, 1965:
    Sutherland, Tyrer, Eadie, Casey and Kurland, 1966:
    McCall, Brereton, Dawson, Milligan, Sutherland and Acheson, 1968:
    McCall, Sutherland and Acheson, 1969:
    Sutherland, 1969:
    Layton and Sutherland, 1974.

TABLE 8

STAFF OF THE DEPARTMENT OF NEUROLOGY AND NEUROSURGERY, 1975

ROYAL BRISBANE HOSPITAL   **UNIVERSITY OF QUEENSLAND**

NEUROLOGY
  VISITING SPECIALISTS
    JM Bradfield (from 1/7/75)   JM Bradfield MB BS, MRACP
                                         (Research Fellow to 31/6/75).
    JL Corbett (to 31/6/75)   MJ Eadie (Part-time Reader)
    MA (Oxon) MB BS, MRCP (UK),   MD, MB BS, PhD, FRACP.
    MRACP, D Phil (Oxon).
    VE Edwards MB BS, FRACP.   JH Tyrer, MB BS, MD,
    PR Mann MB BS, MRCP, FRACP.   MRCP (Lond), FRACP.
    GD Ohlrich (from Oct. 75),
      MB BS, FRACP, MRCP (UK)
    JM Sutherland (to 31/6/75)
      MD (Glasgow),FRCP (Edin),
      FRACP.

  FULL TIME SPECIALISTS
    C Burke (Registrar)   C Lander (Registrar)
    MB BS, MRACP.   MB BS (FRACP Part 1).

NEUROSURGERY
  VISITING SPECIALISTS
    KG Jamieson MD, MS (Melb)
    DS (Qld), FRACS, FACS.
    GS Merry MB BS, FRCS (Eng)
    JDN Yelland MB BS, FRCS
      (Eng), FRACS.

                    FULL TIME SPECIALISTS
    G Stuart (Registrar) MB BS, FRACS.
    J Smith (Registrar) MB BS, FRACS.

215

TABLE 8 (contd)

NEURORADIOLOGY
P Tod MB BS, DR (Syd), FRACR.
A Porter MB BS, DCRA.

NEUROANAESTHETICS
T Brophy MB BS, DA RCP (Lond), RCS (Eng)
FFA, RCS (Eng), FFA, RACS.
DH McConnel MB BS, FFA, RCS (Eng).

NEUROPATHOLOGY
RA Cooke MB BS, DCP (Lond), FRCPA,
MC Path (Lond)

RADIOTHERAPY
KE Mead MB BS, DMRT, RCP (Lond),
RCS (Eng), MRACR, FFR, FRACR.
M Hughes MB BS, MRACR.

ROYAL CHILDREN'S HOSPITAL   **UNIVERSITY OF QUEENSLAND**

NEUROLOGY
DB Appleton BSc, MB BS,   J Pearn (Reader in Child Health)
MRCP, MRACP.   MD, BS, BSc (Qld), PhD (Lond),
                                 FRACP, MRCP (UK), DCH (Lond)

NEUROSURGERY

KJ Jamieson MD, MS (Melb), DS (Qld), FRACS, FACS.
GS Merry MB BS, FRCS (Engl.)
JDN Yelland MB BS, FRCS (Engl.), FRACS.

NURSING STAFF

NEUROLOGY —   Sister A Sypher   (1B) Wards 1B and 2B combined
                                              during alterations to wards.
                     Sister H Steenbergin (2B)
                     (Relieving for 6 months)
                     Sister J Kelsh   (2B)

NEUROSURGERY — Sister J Perrett   (4B)
                Sister F Noble   (4B Theatre)
                Sister P Cay
                (from 31.1.76)

216

Acknowledgements
and References

CHAPTER 1

I am deeply indebted to the following authors and their work:

Churchill WS. *A history of the English speaking peoples.* Vol 1, London: Cassel, 1954.

Lethbridge TC. *The painted men.* London: Melrose, 1954.

Linklater E. *The men of Ness.* London: Cope, 1932.

Magnusson M. *Vikings!* London: The Bodley Head and British Broadcasting Corporation, 1980.

Marwick H. *Orkney.* The county book series. London. Robert Hale. 1951.

Mould DDCP. *West-over-Sea.* Edinburgh . Oliver & Boyd, 1953.

Omand D., ed. *The Caithness Book.* Inverness . Highland Printers. 1972.

Prebble J. *The lion in the north.* London . Secker and Warburg. 1971.

Tomkies M. *My wilderness wildcats.* London. Macdonald and Jane's. Futura. 1978.

Walsh M. *While rivers run.* Edinburgh. Chambers. 1948.

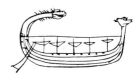

References

CHAPTER 2

My family history was researched by Mrs A Rosemary Bigwood MA, MLitt., genealogist and researcher, 38 Primrose Bank Road, Edinburgh, Scotland, EH5 3JF.

I am particularly indebted to *The Caithness Book*. Omand D., ed., Highland Printers, Inverness 1972, for information regarding Caithness 'Since the '45'. This section was written by Mrs M. Gunn.

I enjoyed refreshing my memory by re-reading the following works:

Churchill WS. *A history of the English speaking people.* Vol. 3. London. Cassel. 1957.

Messenger C. *History of the British Army.* London. Bison Books. 1986.

Prebble J. *The lion in the north.* London. Secker and Warburg. 1971.

Prebble J. *Glencoe: the story of the massacre.* London. Secker and Warburg. 1975.

Taylor IC. *Culloden.* 4 ed. Inverness. Highland Printers for the National Trust for Scotland. 1970.

Thomassen K.
Buist F. *Battles of the '45.* London. Pan Books. 1967.

CHAPTER 3

Hutton P, Gillespie AC, Brown T and McCallum RG., eds. *The High School of Glasgow.* The book of service and remembrance, 1939-45. Glasgow. Aird and Coghill. 1948.

Ashmail HA. *The High School of Glasgow.* Glasgow. Scottish Academic Press. 1976.

Culshaw D, Horrobin P. *The complete catalogue of British cars.* New York. William Morro. 1974.

Wise DB. *The motor car. an illustrated international history.* New York. GP Putman's Sons. 1979.

References

CHAPTER 4

I have always enjoyed reading history and it was a pleasure to re-read and refer to these volumes by Sir Winston Churchill –

The Second World War. Volume 1. 'The gathering storm'. London. The Reprint Society, 1950.

The Second World War. Volume 2. 'Their finest hour'. London. The Reprint Society, 1951.

The Second World War. Volume 3. 'The grand alliance'. London. Cassell and Company, 1950.

I have also referred to –

Churchill RS. 'Into battle'. *Speeches by the Right Hon. Winston Churchill,* compiled by Randolph S. Churchill MP. London. Cassell and Company. 1941.

Kemp, P. ed. Oxford. *The Oxford Companion to Ships and the Sea.* Oxford. Oxford University Press. 1976.

Tute W. *The True Glory: the story of the Royal Navy over a thousand years.* London. Macdonald and Co. 1983.

CHAPTER 5

The Lauderdale Club was formed in 1950. The first Reunion was held 30 September of that year and a Reunion has been held annually since this time. In September, 1979, Volume 1 of 'Lauderdale Remembered: a collection of World War Two anecdotes dredged up by those who served in her' was produced for private circulation to Club members. Three other volumes followed by the final, Volume IV, in 1982, all compiled and edited by Ian Gardiner and produced by Bill Paterson. I have leaned heavily on contributions in these volumes for dates and information. I accept, however, the entire blame for any inaccuracies, plagiarisms and the like.

As ever, *The Oxford Companion to Ships and the Sea* (Kemp PK, ed.) London, Oxford Press, has been an invaluable work of reference. I have also consulted –

Kemp PK. *HM Destroyers.* London. Herbert Jenkins. 1956.

Tute W. *The True Glory: the story of the Royal Navy over 100 years.* London. Macdonald. 1983.

Winton J. *Freedom's Battle.* Vol 1: 'The War at Sea 1939-45'. London. Hutchinson. 1967.

References

CHAPTER 7

The Western Isles of Scotland are, to be accurate, the Outer Hebrides, a chain of islands lying 30–50 miles from the Butt of Lewis in the north to Barra in the south. Nearer the mainland are the Inner Hebrides which include the islands of Skye, Mull, Iona and many more. For those interested I would commend —

MacGregor AA. *The Western Isles.* 2nd ed. London. Robert Hale. 1952.

MacGregor AA. *Skye and the Inner Hebrides.* London. Robert Hale. 1953.

I have refreshed my memory of Flora MacDonald by re-reading —

Wilkins F. *Six Great Scots.* London. Hamish Hamilton. 1961.

Good advice on how to succeed in medicine is given by —

Hawkins CF. 'How to achieve success in medicine.' *Proc.R.Coll.Physic.Edin.* 1988. 161–167.

and on tattooing —

Critchley MacD. 'Tattooed ladies, tattoed men.' **In** *The divine banquet of the brain and other essays.* New York. Raven Press. 1979.

CHAPTER 8

Eadie MJ. Preface. 'Contemporary neurology and neurosurgery'. A symposium. Toowoomba. 1986.

Guthrie D. *Janus in the doorway.* London. Pitman. 1963. 287–297.

Keynes, Sir Geoffrey. 'The Oslerian Tradition'. *Br.Med.J.* 1968. 2. 599–604.

Mayo WJ. 'The John B. Murphy Memorial Building, The Atheneum of Surgery. *Surg.Gynecol.Obstet.* 1926. 43. 256–258.

Tyrer JH. 'The Department of Medicine at Royal Brisbane Hospital.' **In** *: A Medical School for Queensland.* Doherty RL. ed. Brisbane. Boolarong Publications. 1986. 223–239.

References

CHAPTER 9

The following have been consulted in writing this chapter —

Cohen, Lord. *In* Miller, H, ed. 'Early diagnosis.' Edinburgh. Livingstone. 1960.

Doherty RL. (ed) *A Medical School for Queensland.* Brisbane. Boolarong. 1986.

Guthrie D. *Janus in the doorway.* London. Pitman. 1963.

Lock S, Windle H. (eds) 'Remembering Henry'. London. British Medical Association. 1977.

Lorenz KZ. *Man meets dog.* London. Methuen. 1954.

Mackay RP, Wortis SB, Sugar O. *Year Book of Neurology, Psychiatry and Neurosurgery (1964–65 series).* Chicago. Year Book Medical Publishers. 1965.

Osler, Sir William. *Counsels and ideals and selected aphorisms.* Birmingham, Alabama: Classics of Medicine Library. 1985.

Pearn JH. *Focus and Innovation.* A history of paediatric education in Queensland. Brisbane. Dept. of Child Health, University of Queensland. 1986.

The following works have been referred to in the text. They do not constitute a bibliography of papers written by members of the Department of Neurology and Neurosurgery.

Eadie MJ, Tyrer JH, Tod PA, Sutherland JM. 'The diagnosis of tuberose sclerosis.' *Med.J.Aust.* 1962. 547–550.

Eadie MJ, Sutherland JM, Tyrer JH. 'The clinical features of hemifacial atrophy.' *Med.J.Aust.* 1963; 2: 177–180.

Eadie MJ, Tyrer JH, Sutherland JM. 'Significance of extensor plantar responses in muscular dystrophy.' *Arch.Dis.Child* 1963; 38: 13–17.

Eadie MJ. 'Gastric secretion in Parkinsonism.' *Aust.Ann.Med.* 1963. 12: 346-350.

References

CHAPTER 9 (contd)

Eadie MJ. 'The pathology of certain medullary nuclei in Parkinsonism.' *Brain*, 1963; 86: 781–792.

Eadie MJ, Sutherland JM. 'Arteriosclerosis in Parkinsonism.' *J.Neurol.Neurosurg. Psychiatry* 1964; 27: 237–240.

Eadie MJ, Tyrer JH. 'Alimentary disorder in Parkinsonism.' *Aust.Ann.Med.* 1965. 14: 23–27.

Eadie MJ, Sutherland JM, Doherty RL. 'Encephalitis in aetiology of Parkinsonism in Australia.' *Arch.Neurol.* 1965; 12: 240–245.

Eadie MJ, Sutherland JM, Tyrer JH. 'Recurrent monocular blindness of uncertain cause.' *Lancet* 1968. 1: 319–321.

Eadie MJ. 'Hereditary spastic ataxia.' *In:* Vinken and Bruyn eds. *Handbook of clinical neurology.* Amsterdam. North Holland, 1975: 459–465.

Hocking RL, Sampson VE, Sutherland JM. 'Bilateral loss of vision complicating mitral stenosis.' *Med.J.Aust.* 1959. 2: 185–186.

Jamieson KG, Sutherland JM, Yelland JDN. ' Carotico-cavernous sinus fistula with contralateral signs. *Aust.NZ.J.Surg.* 1960; 30. 127–130.

Layton W, Sutherland JM. ' Geochemistry and multiple sclerosis. A hypothesis.' *Med.J.Aust.* 1975; 1: 73–77.

McCall MG, Brerton T Le G, Dawson A, Millingen K, Sutherland JM, Acheson ED 'Frequency of multiple sclerosis in three Australian cities – Perth, Newcastle, Hobart.' *J.Neurol.Neurosurg. Psychiatry* 1968; 31 · 1–9.

McCall MG, Sutherland JM, Acheson ED. 'The frequency of multiple sclerosis in Western Australia.' *Acta Neurol.Scand.* 1969; 45: 151–155.

Miller H. 'Neurology.' *Lancet* 1968; 1: 971–973.

Pearn JH. 'The Florey Fellowship.' See *Focus and Innovation.* Brisbane. Dept of Child Health, University of Queensland 1986. Appendix 4, 525–559.

References

CHAPTER 9 (contd)

Simpson DA, Jamieson KG, Morson SM. 'The foundations of neurourgery in Australia and New Zealand.' *Aust.NZ.J.Surg.* 1974; 44: 215–227.

Sutherland JM, Tyrer JH, Eadie MJ. 'The clinical features of multiple sclerosis.' *Med.J.Aust.* 1961; 1: 49–53.

Sutherland JM, Tyrer JH, Eadie MJ. 'The prevalence of multiple sclerosis in Australia.' *Brain* 1962; 85: 149–164.

Sutherland JM, Tyrer JH, Eadie MJ, Casey JH, Kurland LT. 'The prevalence of multiple sclerosis in Queensland, Australia.' *Acta Neurol.Scand.* 1966; Supp. 19, 41: 57–67.

Sutherland JM, Eadie MJ, Mann PR, Tyrer JH. 'Ancillary investigations in neurological diagnosis.' *Med.J.Aust.* 1967; 2: 542–546.

Sutherland JM, Eadie MJ. 'Cluster headache – migrainous neuralgia.' *In:* Friedmsn AP (ed) *Research and clinical studies in headache.* New York and Basle. Karger, 1971; vol. 3: 92–125.

Sutherland JM. 'Familial spastic paraplegia.' *In:* Vinken and Bruyn eds. *Handbook of clinical neurology.* Amsterdam. North Holland, 1975, Vol. 22. 421–431.

Sutherland JM. 'Certain neuro-ophthalmological aspects of multiple sclerosis.' *Proc.Aust.Ass.Neurol.* 1975. 12: 17–21.

Sutherland JM. 'Doctor at Court.' *Med.J.Aust.* 1979; 2: 355–58.

Tyrer JH, Sutherland JM. 'The primary spino-cerebellar atrophies and their associated defects with a study of the foot deformity.' *Brain* 1961; 84: 289–300.

Tyrer JH, Sutherland JM, Eadie MJ. 'Miosis bilateral dans les deviations voluntaires des yeux dans toute les directions, dans un syndrome de neuromyelite optique.' *Rev.Neurol.* 1963; 109: 72–76.

Tyrer JH. 'Friedreichs ataxia.' *In:* Vinken and Bruyn eds. *Handbook of Clinical Neurology.* Amsterdam. North Holland, 1975, vol. 21: 319–364.

INDEX

Index

Index

Index